Opus 56

Steidle + Partner
Hilmer & Sattler und Albrecht
Ortner und Ortner
Am Bavariapark, München

**Text
Michael Goj
Christoph Tempel**

**Photographien / Photographs
Franziska von Gagern**

Edition Axel Menges

Herausgeber/Editor: Axel Menges

© 2005 Edition Axel Menges, Stuttgart/London
ISBN 3-930698-56-0

Alle Rechte vorbehalten, besonders die der Übersetzung in andere Sprachen.
All rights reserved, especially those of translation into other languages.

Druck und Bindearbeiten/Printing and binding:
Daehan Printing & Publishing Co., Ltd., Sungnam, Korea

Übersetzung ins Englische/Translation into English:
Michael Robinson
Design: Axel Menges

Inhalt

6 Michael Goj, Christoph Tempel: Wohnen am Bavariapark
18 Pläne
   Übersichtsplan 18 – Lageplan 19 – Grundrisse 20 – Schnitte 22 – Ansichten 24
26 Bildteil
   Gesamtansicht 26 – Detailansichten 28
60 Daten

Contents

7 Michael Goj, Christoph Tempel: Living by the Bavariapark
18 Plans
   General plan 18 – Site plan 19 – Floor plans 20 – Sections 22 – Elevations 24
26 Pictorial section
   General view 26 – Detailed views 28
60 Credits

Michael Goj, Christian Tempel
Wohnen am Bavariapark

»Den besten Blick aufs Gelände habt ihr aus dem Café-Restaurant ›Westend‹«, gab uns ein Münchner Freund mit auf den Weg. Das ist eines jener Ecklokale mit großen Schaufenstern, wie sie sonst eher in Berlin anzutreffen sind. Mit Berlin kennen wir uns aus, von dort haben wir uns auf den Weg gemacht zur Theresienhöhe, einem der großen innerstädtischen Entwicklungsgebiete der bayerischen Landeshauptstadt. Wir sind hier, um das Kernstück des neuen Stadtteils zu beschreiben, die nach ihrer Lage »Esplanade« oder »Am Bavariapark« genannte Mischung aus Wohn- und Bürobauten zwischen Ganghoferstraße und Bavariapark, die im Zusammenwirken dreier Architekturbüros entstanden ist: Ortner & Ortner Baukunst, Wien/Berlin, Hilmer & Sattler und Albrecht, München, sowie der Verfasser des Masterplans Otto Steidle + Partner, München.

Den guten Kilometer vom Hauptbahnhof haben wir zu Fuß zurückgelegt und kurz vor dem Ziel erstaunt die winterlich wüste Theresienwiese überquert: Nichts erinnert an die bierselige Hochsaison im Oktober, und selbst die Bavaria wirkt blaß und verfroren.

Oben auf der Hangkante empfängt uns ein Phänomen, das man in München noch nicht lange kennt: Leerstand. Der fünfteilige Büro-, Geschäfts- und Wohnkomplex »Theresie« der Braunschweiger Architekten KSP Engel und Zimmermann und erstes Einzelwettbewerbsergebnis der Theresienhöhe wartet auf Mieter, auf die ihrerseits ein grandioser Blick über die Freifläche der Theresienwiese wartet.

An den dahinter liegenden drei denkmalgeschützten Messehallen von Wilhelm Bertsch (1907/08) im Zentrum der Theresienhöhe wird noch gebaut, die Wege sind versperrt. Von der Heimeranstraße gelangen wir auf die Ganghoferstraße, die zentrale Erschließungsachse des Entwicklungsgebiets, repräsentativer Mittelpunkt und Anknüpfung an die angrenzende Wohnbebauung. Hier befindet sich das Café-Restaurant »Westend«, das seinen Namen von dem Münchner Stadtbezirk entliehen hat, in dem es sich befindet.

Westend

»Westend – Vom Fortschritt umzingelt« überschreibt der kürzlich erschienene *München Atlas* das Kapitel über den traditionellen Arbeiterbezirk und bringt den Wandel des kleinsten und mit 104 Einwohnern pro Hektar gegenüber dem Münchner Durchschnitt von 42 Einwohnern dichtest besiedelten Stadtteils der bayerischen Landeshauptstadt auf den Punkt. »Durch große Neubauvorhaben wird das Westend heute von hochwertigen Nutzungen eingekreist. Diese Entwicklung begann entlang der Bahnlinie zum Ostbahnhof (Landsberger Straße, Barthstraße, Riedlerstraße bis zur Ganghoferstraße). Am früheren Standort der Hackerbrauerei wurden attraktive Bürogebäude geschaffen, in denen unter anderem das Europäische Patentamt seinen Sitz gefunden hat. Daran anschließend wird im Zuge der Revitalisierung der Bahnflächen zwischen Hauptbahnhof und Pasing auch das Gelände des ehemaligen Milchladehofs überplant.«

Wir befinden uns im östlichen Teil vom Westend, auf der Theresienhöhe, und die hat ihre eigene Geschichte. Um eine Verbauung des in der Mitte des 19. Jahrhunderts von König Ludwig I. auf der Theresienhöhe errichteten Ensembles von Bavaria-Statue und Ruhmeshalle durch profane Wohnviertel zu verhindern, wurde von den Wittelsbachern die Idee eines Ausstellungs- und Vergnügungsparks protegiert. Dessen Mitte bildete der etwa 24 ha große, 1908 eröffnete Bavariapark, als Vergnügungspark 1934 wieder geschlossen. Von da an vollzog sich allmählich und, nach dem Zweiten Weltkrieg durch die Gründung der Münchner Messe- und Ausstellungsgesellschaft beschleunigt, die Entwicklung in ein modernes, internationalen Ansprüchen genügen-

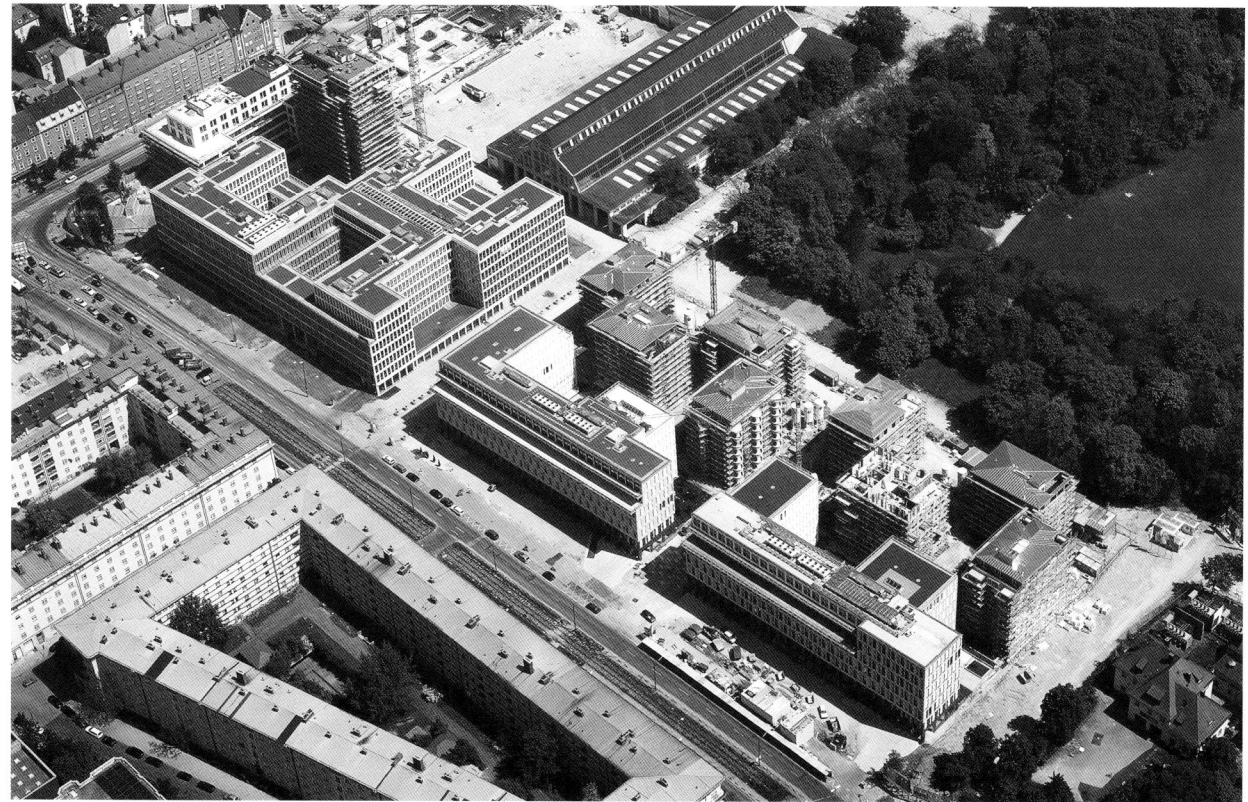

1. Luftaufnahme des Geländes. Oben links das KPMG-Gebäude, rechts sich daran anschließend die beiden Kontorhäuser Nord und Süd und die acht Wohnblocks. (Photo: Reinhard Görner.)

1. Aerial view of the site. On the top left the KPMG building, to the right of it the north and south office buildings and the eight apartment blocks. (Photo: Reinhard Görner.)

Michael Goj, Christian Tempel
Living by the Bavariapark

»You get the best view of the site form the ›Westend‹ café-restaurant«, was the advice from a Munich friend as we set off. It's one of those corner establishments with big windows of the kind you tend to see more in Berlin. We know our way around Berlin, that's where we set off from to visit the Theresienhöhe, one of the Bavarian capital's biggest inner-city development areas. We're here to describe the centrepiece of this new district. It is a mixture of residential and offices buildings between Ganghoferstraße and the Bavariapark called »Esplanade« or »Am Bavariapark« according to location. It was designed by three architectural practices working together: Ortner & Ortner Baukunst, Vienna/Berlin, Hilmer & Sattler und Albrecht, Munich, and the author of the master plan Otto Steidle + Partner, Munich.

We walked the good kilometre from the main station, and were astonished as we crossed the wintery desert of the Theresienwiese just before our destination: not a sign of the beery high season at the Oktoberfest, and even the statue of Bavaria herself looks pale and frozen stiff.

At the top on the edge of the slope we are met by a phenomenon that is relatively new to Munich: empty property. The five-part office, commercial and residential »Theresie« complex by the Braunschweig architects KSP Engel und Zimmermann, the first individual competition result on the Theresienhöhe, is still waiting for tenants. Waiting for them in their turn is a magnificent view over the open spaces of the Theresienwiese.

Building work is still in progress on the three listed exhibition halls (1907/08) by Wilhelm Bertsch at the centre of the Theresienhöhe, and the roads are closed. Heimeranstraße takes us into Ganghoferstraße, the central access road for the development area, prestigious central point and a link with the adjacent residential development. Here is the »Westend« café-restaurant, which takes its name from the Munich district it is located in.

Westend

»Westend – encircled by progress« was the heading chosen for the chapter on this traditional working-class area for the recently published *München Atlas*. It sums up the changes that have occurred in Munich's smallest and yet most densely populated district, with 104 inhabitants per hectare against the Munich average of 42. »Major new building projects mean that Westend is now being surrounded by high-quality developments. These began along the railway line to the Ostbahnhof (Landsberger Straße, Barthstraße, Riedlerstraße to Ganghoferstraße). Attractive office premises have been built on the former Hackerbräu brewery site, now accommodating the European Patent Office headquarters, among others. Adjacent to this, new plans are also in hand for the former dairy loading yard, as part of the revitalization of the railway land between the main station and Pasing.«

We are in the eastern part of Westend, on the Theresienhöhe, and this has a history of its own. To avoid reducing the impact of the ensemble of Bavaria statue and Hall of Fame, built on the Theresienhöhe in the mid 19th century by King Ludwig I, with mundane housing projects, the Wittelsbachs supported the idea of an exhibition and leisure park. At the centre of this was the Bavariapark, which opened in 1909 and was closed as a leisure park in 1934. From then on a modern exhibition site of international calibre started to emerge, and this process was accelerated by the foundation of the Münchner Messe- und Ausstellungsgesellschaft after the Second World War. The end of this chapter came in 1998, with the start of the Munich exhibition centre's move to the former Riem airport site, and the 100-year-old idea of a new urban quarter gained its second chance.

There was agreement from the outset that the new quarter should be a compact inner-city development with an independent character, but nevertheless one that should be integrated into the surrounding area. A mixture of offices, homes, commerce and services was decided upon, always assuming urban quality and a high standard for the development measures. Otto Steidle's master plan was accepted in the multi-stage urban development process that was set in train in 1996, accompanied by a special commission including all local government offices, an expert »urban-design committee« and the »Theresienhöhe working party«, which was open to all citizens.

The Theresienhöhe site occupies about 45 ha, and will contain approx. 200 000 m² of office space and 14 000 m² of commercial premises, overall about 5 000 workplaces, 1 500 dwellings and also schools, kindergartens and youth centres. The Deutsches Museum is to move its Transport Centre into the three remaining former exhibition halls, which will restore the link with the sites original use for trade fair purposes.

The raw and the cooked

The Café Westend has a grandstand view of the KPMG building and accompanying office blocks, and here we turned our attention to the simple one-course meals with accompanying salad that were on offer. The raw and the cooked came together on the table and suggested some observations that Erich Wiesner, Otto Steidle's long-standing friend and »colour-man« had offered us as an explanation in Berlin. For him this contrasting pair, borrowed from Claude Lévi-Strauss and standing for interlinking of culture and nature in myth, is equally useful for defining the interplay between construction, material and colour in the three large office buildings on the Ganghoferstraße esplanade. Here we have the extraordinarily lively façade of the KPMG building, dissolved into colour and glass, and there the two large, calm façades of the office buildings with their serenely alternating narrow and wide wall apertures and subdued colours intended to be reminiscent of the sandy pictorial surfaces of an artist like Antoni Tàpies or the Plaza Mayor in Salamanca.

Steidle wrote this about Erich Wiesner in the catalogue for his »Land Stadt Haus« exhibition: »We work together on the design concept, with boundaries that are fluid, but not blurred. The seclusion of his Kreuzberg studio gives him a different freedom but also a greater intensity in relation to the individual elements, colour, texture and light. I work from the order imposed by the great structure of the city and the building, while

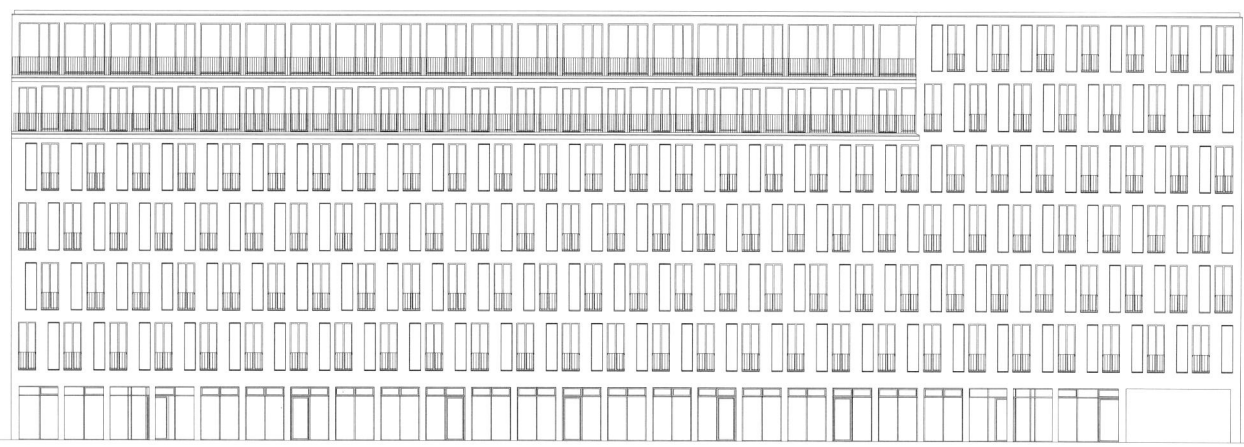

des Messegelände. Mit der Anfang 1998 abgeschlossenen Verlegung der Messe München auf das Flugfeld des früheren Flughafens Riem war dieses Kapitel beendet, und der 100 Jahre alte Grundgedanke der Entwicklung eines neuen Stadtquartiers erhielt seine zweite Chance.

Von Beginn an war man sich darin einig, daß das neue Viertel eine kompakte innerstädtische Bebauung mit eigenständigem Charakter erhalten und sich dennoch in das benachbarte Umfeld integrieren sollte. Eine Mischung aus Büros, Wohnen, Handel und Dienstleistung wurde festgeschrieben, Urbanität und eine gewisse Hochwertigkeit der Entwicklungsmaßnahmen stets voraussetzend. In dem 1996 in Gang gesetzten mehrstufigen städtebaulichen Verfahren, das von einer ämterübergreifenden Fachkommission, einem expertenbestückten »Beirat Stadtgestaltung« sowie dem allen Bürgern offenstehenden »Arbeitskreis Theresienhöhe« begleitet wurde, konnte sich Otto Steidle mit seinem Masterplan durchsetzen.

Auf den etwa 45 ha der Theresienhöhe entstehen ca. 200 000 m² Bürofläche und 14 000 m² Gewerberaum, insgesamt an die 5 000 Arbeitsplätze, 1 500 Wohnungen sowie Schulen, Kindergärten und Jugendzentren. Mit dem Einzug des Verkehrszentrums des Deutschen Museums in die drei verbliebenen ehemaligen Messehallen wird wieder an die ursprüngliche Nutzung als Ort von Ausstellungen angeknüpft.

Das Rohe und das Gekochte

Im Café »Westend« mit Logenblick auf das KPMG-Gebäude und die sogenannten Kontorhäuser widmen wir uns den angebotenen einfachen Tellergerichten mit Salatbeilage. Das Rohe und das Gekochte vereinen sich auf dem Tisch und regen zu Betrachtungen an, die Erich Wiesner, langjähriger Freund und »Färber« Otto Steidles, uns in Berlin als Erklärung angeboten hat. Für ihn bezeichnet dieses Claude Lévi-Strauss entlehnte Gegensatzpaar, das für die Verschränkung von Kultur und Natur im Mythos steht, gleichermaßen das Zusammenspiel von Konstruktion, Material und Farbigkeit bei den drei großen Bürohäusern an der Esplanade Ganghoferstraße. Hier die außerordentlich bewegte Front des KPMG-Gebäudes, aufgelöst in Farbe und Glas, dort die beiden ruhigen Großformen der Kontorhäuser mit dem unaufgeregten Wechsel von schmalen und breiteren Wandöffnungen und den gedeckten Farben, die an die sandigen Bildoberflächen eines Antoni Tàpies oder die Plaza Mayor von Salamanca erinnern sollen.

Steidle schreibt im Katalog zu seiner Ausstellung »Land Stadt Haus« über Erich Wiesner: »Wir arbeiten gemeinsam am Gestaltungskonzept mit fließenden, aber nicht verwischten Grenzen. Aus der Abgeschiedenheit seines Kreuzberger Ateliers heraus ist ihm eine andere Freiheit, aber auch eine stärkere Intensität in bezug auf das einzelne Element, die Farbe, die Textur und das Licht gegeben. Während ich von den Ordnungen der großen Gefüge der Stadt und des Gebäudes komme, ist er mit Phänomenen der sinnlichen, objekthaften und mentalen Ebenen beschäftigt. Während ich unsere Entwürfe den Behörden und Investoren auf allen Ebenen vermittle und sie vor verlustreichen Eingriffen schützen muß, baut er Assoziationsketten aus dem Bereich einer zeitgenössischen oder weltweiten oder regionalen Kunst auf.«

Das Lackierte und das Trockene, das Besondere und das Alltägliche: Die Liste der Gegensatzpaare ließe sich nach Belieben erweitern, wobei im Büro Steidle das Besondere nicht zwangsläufig immer das Bessere sein muß. Schließlich belehrt Otto Steidle seine Studentinnen und Studenten an der Akademie der Bildenden Künste in München, daß nicht immer Sonntag sein kann. »Im Leben nicht und auch nicht in der Architektur, erst recht nicht im Städtebau.« Und hinsichtlich der drei Bürogebäude an der Esplanade hebt man im Büro Steidle die Normalität der beiden südlichen, der Kontorhäuser, als Wert hervor: »Die Innovation besteht vielleicht darin, daß sie ganz normal funktionieren.«

»Die Fassaden der Kontorhäuser«, sagt Otto Steidle, »sollen zwar eigenständig sein, sich jedoch zugunsten des städtischen Charakters nicht besonders hervortun.« Die Fassadengliederung bedient sich dazu der klassischen Unterteilung in Sockel-, Mittel- und Dachzone und differenziert diese Themen nicht nur durch plastisch hervortretende, sondern auch durch fassadenbündige breitere und schmalere Fenstertüren. Die Farben der gemauerten Keramikfassade folgen dem Aufbau: dunkel die Sockel, sandfarben die fein gezeichneten Mittelzonen und hell der obere Abschluß. Das eigentümliche »Flimmern« der Fassade verdankt sich dem Einsatz von drei leicht abgestuften Steinfarben und deren diagonalem Versatz im Mauerwerksverband.

Was auf den ersten Blick bei beiden Häusern gleich erscheint, zeigt beim genauen Hinsehen feine Nuancierungen. Beim südlichen Kontorhaus etwa setzt sich das Anthrazit des Sockels in den dunkel eingefärbten Fensterlaibungen aus Metall in der Mittelzone fort, die beiden Staffelgeschosse sind verputzt und nicht über die gesamte Front geführt, so daß sie wie in die Fassade eingelassen erscheinen. Beim zweiten Kontorhaus sind die

2. Steidle + Partner, Kontorhaus Süd. Aufriß der Westseite.
3. Steidle + Partner, Kontorhäuser Nord und West. Fassadendetails.
4. Steidle + Partner, Kontorhaus Nord. (Photo: Franziska von Gagern.)

2. Steidle + Partner, south office building. West elevation.
3. Steidle + Partner, north and south office buildings. Façade details.
4. Steidle + Partner, north office building. (Photo: Franziska von Gagern.)

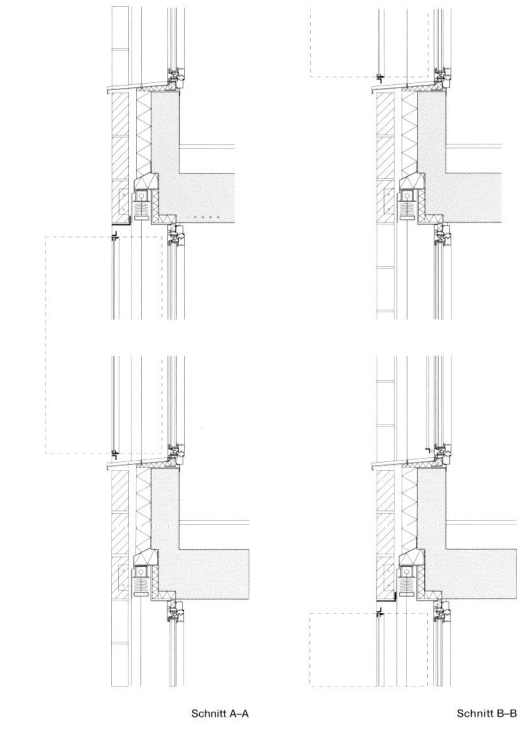

Schnitt A–A   Schnitt B–B

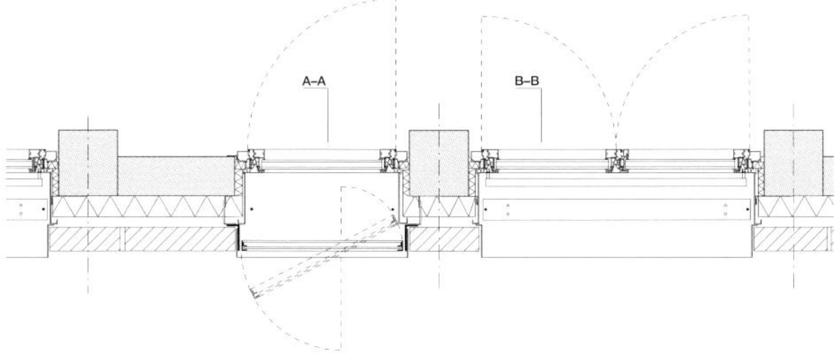

he concerns himself with phenomena deriving from the sensual, object-related and intellectual planes. I convey our designs to the authorities and developers on all planes and have to protect them from damaging interventions, while he builds chains of association from the field of contemporary or world-wide or regional art.«

Painted and unpainted, special and ordinary: the list of contrasting pairs could be extended at will, though in the Steidle practice special does not necessarily mean better. We have to remember that Otto Steidle teaches his students at the Akademie der Bildenden Künste in Munich that it cannot always be Sunday. »Not in life, and not in architecture either, and certainly not in urban development.« And when talking about the three office buildings on the Esplanade, in the Steidle practice the ordinariness of the two office buildings south of the KPMG building is seen as positive: »The innovative element might be that they work quite normally.«

»The façades of the office buildings«, says Otto Steidle, »are certainly intended to be independent, but they should not assert themselves unduly in terms of urban character.« To achieve this, the façades are structured using the classical division into base, middle and roof zone, distinguishing between them not only with three-dimensionally modelled tall windows in the shape of french doors, but also with some wider and narrower windows fitting flush with the façade. The colours of the masonry ceramic façades follow the structure: dark bases, a sandy shade for the finely marked middle zones, and light colours for the top. The façade seems to »shimmer« because three gently graded stone colours are used, set diagonally into the pattern of the brickwork.

The two buildings may look identical at first glance, but nuances emerge on closer examination. In the south building, for example, the anthracite of the base continues in the dark-coloured metal window reveals in the middle zone, the two staggered floors are rendered and do not extend across the whole façade, so that they look as though they have been set into it. In the second office building the window reveals are sandy-coloured on the main floors and again anthracite in the staggered storeys. This, supported by the different-sized windows, creates a strange tension and sense of linkage in the façade of each of the office buildings, but also between the two of them.

Each office building has two corner entrances, with underground car park access near the south entrance. The simple designed entrance halls derive their vigour from three ideas: a centrally positioned black column, the offset staircase and the colour scheme. Instead of hiding the stairs, which in offices are increasingly being reduced to mere escape routes, behind the lift, the architects stage a small »promenade architecturale« that takes staircase users from the hall into the transverse section of the building and back into the hall from there.

The two strong colours in Erich Wiesner's square, vertically divided glass pictures in the 4.2 by 4.2 m format both reinforce and temper the light. The upper floors follow the conventional pattern with offices on either side of a central corridor. Kitchens, wider corridors as communication areas, everything has its place. But attention should be drawn to a simple yet effective idea for the windows. Because noise pollution is high and it was decided that there should be no air conditioning, an easily managed ventilation flap was needed. Now there are normal two-leaved windows set deep in the wall, and next to them is a narrow, flush vent in a box-type window with an aperture at the top and the bottom providing adequate ventilation with minimum noise.

But things do become spectacular in the two staggered storeys, though the ground plans are no different – spectacular because of the broad terraces in front of the offices. Although it is draughty and cold on this winter's day we didn't want to come down from this viewing platform. Seen from up here, the 1920s blocks opposite, which seem so solid and closed from below, open up. The northern one is from the pen of Theodor Fischer. It is possible to see into the yards, and the top storey of the Fischer building, which has loggias looking inwards, becomes visible. The interesting roof behind it belongs to a school, we are told, and that Otto Steidle attended it for a year or so, but that isn't particularly important here.

As Winfried Nerdinger points out, Otto Steidle always stressed when talking about Theodor Fischer's hostel for unmarried people dating from 1927, which is only a few steps from here in Bergmannstraße, »how this great urban developer picked up the block structure of the surrounding development, but also took the liberty of opening up this block and using a higher section of the building to provide a new signal for future projects in this district«. Steidle's urban development plans for Theresienhöhe show that he learned from Theodor Fischer with the positioning of the »Park Plaza« high-rise apartments behind the KPMG building, and even earlier – admittedly on a quite different scale – with his design for Potsdamer Platz in Berlin, in which he placed towers inside the block, to ward off any sense of monumentality. But there are also echoes of Theodor Fischer's hostel architecture in the façade articulation and in the treatment of the building masses for the three large office buildings in Ganghoferstraße, most clearly in the case of the KPMG building.

Ganghoferstraße esplanade

At the time of writing the contrast between the KPMG building and the two office blocks is still very striking, but it will be reduced with the passage of time, at the latest when the three planned rows of trees screen off the view of the buildings. So it is not possible to form a final impression, as the Esplanade is still emerging. It extends in a wedge-shape over 400 m from the railway bridge at the south end to Heimeranstraße in the north, its width constantly expanding from 21 to 37 m, or 47 m in the section with a tree-lined square. At the time of writing it takes some imagination to imagine Ganghoferstraße, fringed with building sites as it is, as the linear open space intended by the Berlin landscape architects Thomanek + Duquesnoy as an attractive way into the new urban quarter. The light-coloured natural stone flags in the square format borrowed from Munich's Ludwigstraße is still missing, with a band of contrasting dark natural stone, out of which will grow »rhythmically spaced seating of various sizes, facing first one side, and then the other«. The landscape architects explain that material quality and furnishings are used to make a reticent yet imposing impression ap-

Fensterlaibungen in den Hauptgeschossen sandfarben und in den Staffelgeschossen erneut anthrazit. So entsteht, unterstützt von den unterschiedlichen Fenstergrößen, eine eigentümliche Spannung und Verzahnung in der Fassade eines jeden der beiden Kontorhäuser, aber auch untereinander.

An den Ecken öffnen sich je Kontorhaus zwei Eingänge, neben dem Südeingang liegt eine Tiefgarageneinfahrt. Die einfach gestalteten Eingangshallen leben von drei Einfällen: einer zentral positionierten schwarzen Säule, dem Versatz des Treppenlaufs und der Farbgebung. Anstatt die in Bürohäusern zunehmend zum reinen Fluchtweg verkommenden Treppen hinter dem Fahrstuhl zu verstecken, inszenieren die Architekten eine kleine »promenade architecturale«, die den Treppengänger von der Halle in den Querriegel des Gebäudes und von dort wieder in die Halle zurückführt.

Die beiden kräftigen Farben der quadratischen, vertikal geteilten Glasbilder von Erich Wiesner im Format 4,20 x 4,20 m verstärken und temperieren das Licht. Die oberen Geschosse sind konventioneller Bürobau mit zweihüftig angeordneten, von einem zentralen Flur erschlossenen Büros. Teeküchen, aufgeweitete Flure als Orte der Kommunikation, alles hat seinen Platz. Hervorzuheben ist jedoch die einfache und effektive Lösung für die Fenster. Wegen der hohen Lärmbelastung und dem Verzicht auf Klimatisierung des Gebäudes bedurfte es einer Art leicht zu handhabender Lüftungsflügel. Jetzt gibt es normale, tief in der Wand sitzende zweiflügelige Fenster und daneben einen schmalen, plan angebrachten Flügel in einem Kastenfenster, dessen Spalte oben und unten ausreichende Luftzufuhr bei geringer Lärmbelastung ermöglicht.

In den beiden Staffelgeschossen wird es dann doch noch spektakulär, wobei die Grundrisse sich nicht weiter unterscheiden – spektakulär wegen der breiten Terrassen vor den Büroräumen. Obwohl es zugig und kalt ist an diesem Wintertag, wollen wir gar nicht wieder hinunter von dieser Aussichtsplattform. Von hier oben öffnen sich die gegenüberliegenden, von unten so fest und geschlossen wirkenden Blöcke aus den 1920er Jahren, der nördliche aus der Feder von Theodor Fischer. Einblicke in die Höfe werden möglich, das nach innen mit Loggien geöffnete Dachgeschoß des Fischerbaus wird sichtbar. Das interessante Dach dahinter gehört zu einer Schule, erklärt man uns, und daß Otto Steidle da mal ein Jahr oder so hingegangen sei, aber das spielt hier eigentlich keine Rolle.

Wie Winfried Nerdinger zu berichten weiß, hat Otto Steidle am Beispiel von Theodor Fischers Ledigenheim aus dem Jahr 1927, das nur wenige Schritte von hier entfernt in der Bergmannstraße liegt, betont, »wie dieser große Städtebauer zum einen die Blockgliederung der umgebenden Bebauung aufgriff, sich aber zum anderen die Freiheit nahm, diesen Block zu öffnen und mit einem höheren Bauteil auch ein ganz neues Zeichen für zukünftige Entwicklungen in diesem Stadtteil zu setzen«. Daß Steidle von Theodor Fischer gelernt hat, beweist sein städtebaulicher Entwurf auf der Theresienhöhe auch mit der Positionierung des »Park Plaza«-Wohnturms hinter dem KPMG-Gebäude und schon früher – freilich in anderem Maßstab – mit dem Entwurf für den Potsdamer Platz in Berlin, bei dem er zur Abwehr jeglicher Monumentalität Türme ins Blockinnere plazierte. Anklänge an Theodor Fischers Architektur des Ledigenheims finden sich aber auch in der Fassadengliederung wie in der Behandlung der Baumassen der drei großen Bürogebäude an der Ganghoferstraße, am deutlichsten am KPMG-Gebäude.

Esplanade Ganghoferstraße

Der derzeit noch auffallende Gegensatz zwischen dem KPMG-Gebäude und den beiden Kontorhäusern wird sich im Lauf der Zeit verschleifen, spätestens dann, wenn die drei geplanten Baumreihen den Blick auf die Gebäude abschirmen werden. Deshalb kann auch unser Eindruck von der Situation kein endgültiger sein, denn die Esplanade ist noch im Werden. Sie erstreckt sich keilförmig über 400 m von der Eisenbahnbrücke im Süden zur Heimeranstraße im Norden, mit stetig wachsender Breite von 21 bis 37 m beziehungsweise 47 m im Bereich des Baumplatzes. Augenblicklich bedarf es einiger Vorstellungskraft, um sich die von Baustellen gesäumte Ganghoferstraße als diesen linearen Freiraum vorzustellen, den die Berliner Landschaftsarchitekten Thomanek+Duquesnoy als attraktives Entree für das neue Stadtquartier vorsehen. Noch fehlt der helle Natursteinbelag im rechteckigen Ludwigstraßenformat, von dem sich ein Band aus dunklem Naturstein absetzen soll und dem in »rhythmischen Abständen Sitzelemente, variierend in der Größe und mit wechselnder Orientierung zu einer der beiden Seiten« entwachsen werden. Materialität und Ausstattung werden, dem Charakter der angrenzenden Bürobebauung angemessen, zum Zwecke zurückhaltender Repräsentanz eingesetzt, erläutern die Landschaftsarchitekten. Man wird sehen, ob es der angestammten Nachbarschaft gelingen wird, sich diese großzügigen, repräsentativ gestalteten öffentlichen Räume zu eigen zu machen.

Der aufgelöste Block

»Der städtebauliche Entwurf für die Theresienhöhe bezieht sich konzeptionell auf die Kontinuität der gewachsenen europäischen Stadt, auf deren Charakteristika und historische Spuren, und integriert diese mit Varianten der Bauelemente Block, Zeile, Punkt in eine neue Form urbaner Zusammenhänge.« Otto Steidle ist weder der Versuchung erlegen, die vorgefundene Blockrandstruktur zu kopieren, wie es am Planungsprozeß beteiligte Bürger wegen der Einbindung ins angrenzende Westend nahegelegt hatten, noch wollte er die Stadt neu erfinden. Er will die Stadt fortschreiben, wiederentdecken, neu entwickeln. »Auf der Theresienhöhe bin ich beim Städtebau zunächst einmal einer These gefolgt, die ich aus einem anderen Bereich übernommen habe. Ich sagte nämlich: Beim Städtebau darf man alles haben, nur keine Idee!«

Gefragt sei zunächst eine stabile Ausstattung der Stadt. »Das reicht von guten, funktionierenden Straßen – die, wenn sie gut sind, mit und ohne Autos auch öffentliche Räume darstellen – bis hin zu einer Verfügungsfläche, auf der unterschiedliche Architekten ihre verschiedenen Ideen zum Haus realisieren, denn diese Ideen muß man nicht vorgeben. Diese Verfügungsflächen gehen also nicht von den einzelnen Häusern aus und folgen auch nicht jedem einzelnen Haus. Das war eines meiner Grundprinzipien: Sie sollen viel Freiheit ermöglichen. Davor muß man sich aber eben auf ein verbindliches Maß, auf verbindliche Größenordnun-

5. Steidle+Partner, Wettbewerbsprojekt. Lageplan.
6. Hilmer & Sattler und Albrecht, Wettbewerbsprojekt. Lageplan.
7. Ortner & Ortner, Wettbewerbsprojekt. Lageplan.
8. Hilmer & Sattler und Albrecht, Wettbewerbsprojekt. Perspektive.

5. Steidle+Partner, competition project. Site plan.
6. Hilmer & Sattler und Albrecht, competition project. Site plan.
7. Ortner & Ortner, competition project. Site plan.
8. Hilmer & Sattler und Albrecht, competition project. Perspective drawing.

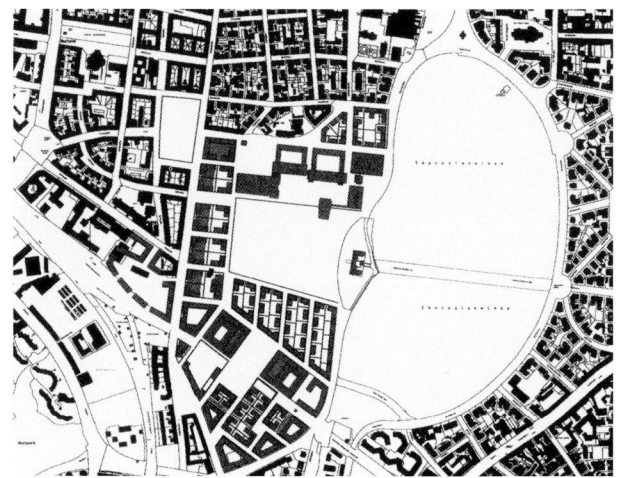

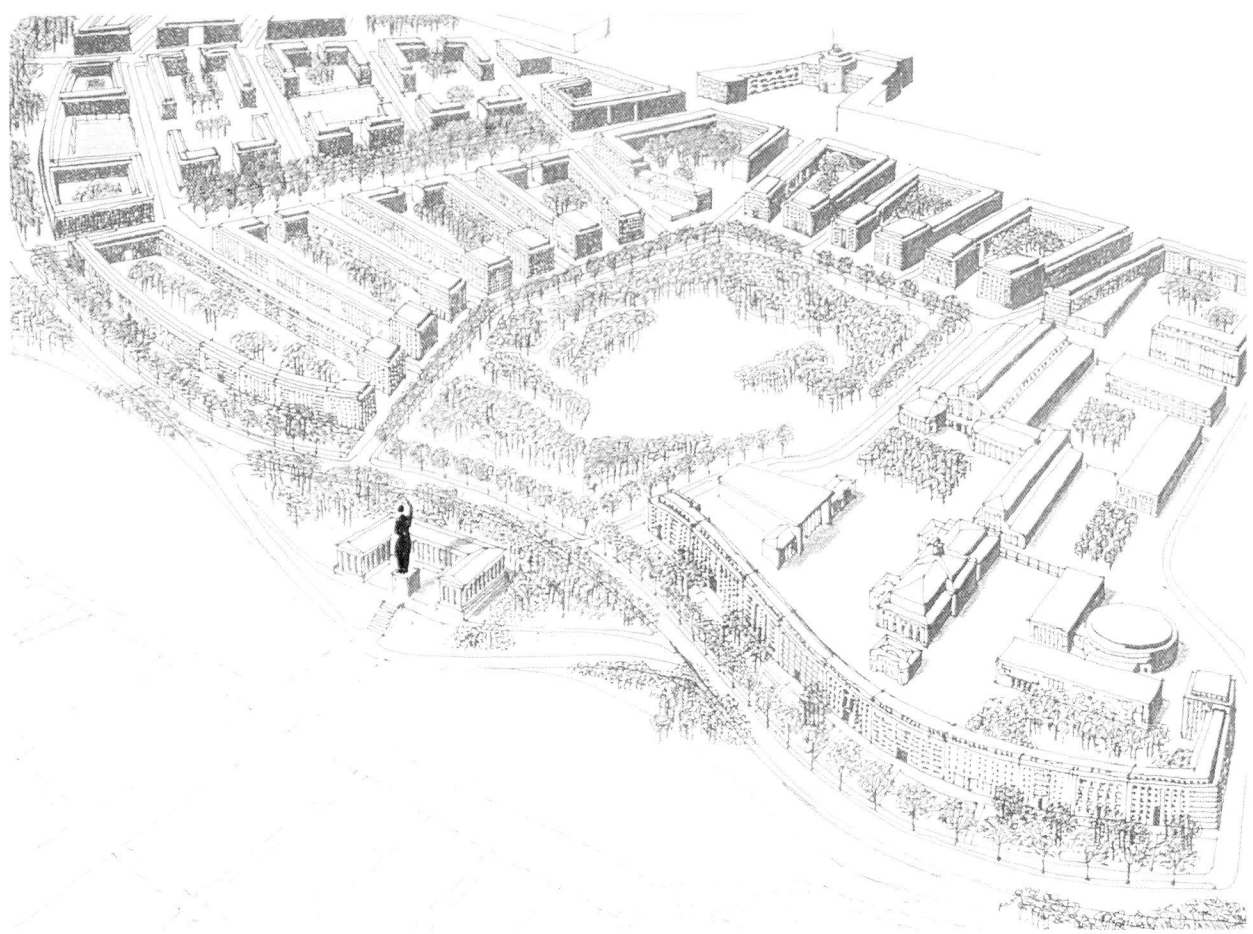

propriate to the character of the adjacent office development. It remains to be seen whether the established neighbours will be able to make these generously scaled, prestigiously designed public spaces their own.

The dissolved block

»The urban development design for Theresienhöhe relates conceptually to the continuity of the naturally evolved European city, to its characteristics and historical traces, and integrates this with variants on the building elements block, row and point in a new approach to urban connections.« Otto Steidle has not yielded to the temptation to copy the existing block structure, as citizens involved in the planning process had urged, with an eye to linking up with adjacent Westend, and he was also not trying to re-invent the city. He wants to continue the city, rediscover it, redevelop it. »On the Theresienhöhe I first followed a thesis for my urban development that I took over from another sphere. In fact I said: in urban development you can have everything, except an idea!«

The first aim is stable provision for the city. »This extends from good roads that work well – if they are good they are public spaces, with or without cars – to an area that is at the disposal of different architects to realize their various ideas about buildings: these ideas must not be prescribed. So the areas at their disposal do not start with individual buildings, and they do not follow each individual building either. That was one of my basic principles: they should offer a great deal of freedom. But before that you have to have committed yourself to an obligatory scale, to obligatory sizes, to obligatory open spaces. ... Things are similar on the Theresienhöhe: there are certain principles representing principles of public urban space that have been developed further and modified, and that have to be respected.«

The starting-point for his design is the attempt to »formulate a new urban structure for the former exhibition site from the module of the surrounding quarters, without copying them«, as the jury recognized. Reinterpreting the block as a »dissolved block« is the guiding image, with each block fundamentally providing stable peripheries for the public park in terms of perspective. The jury felt that this reinterpretation brought with it »a quality that achieves both integration into the surrounding area and an independent quality for the quarter«. A dialogue between block, point and row is sought for reasons of use (light, air, sun, green), and yet an urban character should dominate at all times.

Another characteristic the jury found in Steidle's block grid was the possibility of admitting different urban and architectural spatial structures and images, along with successive growth and different architectural handwriting.

The two designs that came second and third in the 1996 urban development competition, by Hilmer & Sattler und Albrecht, Munich, with landscape architects Latz & Partner, Kranzberg, and Ortner & Ortner, Vienna/Berlin, with landscape architects Burger + Tischer, Munich, show a different approach to the development area.

The jury said that the design by Hilmer & Sattler und Albrecht appealed »through the idea of capturing the curve of the ice-age edge of the Isar slope in a development«. The jury found another sign of quality »in the relationship between the development and the park«:

gen, auf verbindliche öffentliche Räume eingelassen haben. ... So ähnlich ist es auch auf der Theresienhöhe: Es gibt bestimmte Prinzipien, die weiterentwickelte, modifizierte Prinzipien des öffentlichen städtischen Raums darstellen und die eingehalten werden müssen.«

Ausgangspunkt seines Entwurfs ist der Versuch, eine »neue stadträumliche Struktur für das ehemalige Messegelände aus dem Modul der umliegenden Quartiere zu formulieren, ohne diese zu kopieren«, wie die Jury erkannte. Die Neuinterpretation des Blocks als »aufgelöster Block« ist das Leitbild, wobei grundsätzlich jeder Block perspektivisch stabile Kanten zum öffentlichen Park hin ausbildet. In dieser Neuinterpretation sah die Jury eine »Qualität, die sowohl die Integration in die Umgebung wie die Eigenständigkeit des Quartiers leistet«. Aus Nutzungsgründen (Licht, Luft, Sonne, Grün) wird der Dialog von Block, Punkt und Zeile gesucht, dennoch soll durchgängig ein urbaner Charakter vorherrschend sein.

Als weiteres Merkmal erkannte die Jury im Steidleschen Blockraster die Möglichkeit, unterschiedliche städtebauliche und architektonische Raumstrukturen und Erscheinungsbilder zuzulassen sowie sukzessives Wachstum und unterschiedliche architektonische Handschriften zu ermöglichen.

Eine andere städtebauliche Herangehensweise an das Entwicklungsgebiet zeigen die Entwürfe der beiden im städtebaulichen Ideenwettbewerb von 1996 zweit- und drittplazierten Büros Hilmer & Sattler und Albrecht, München, mit den Landschaftsarchitekten Latz + Partner, Kranzberg, und Ortner & Ortner, Wien/Berlin, mit den Landschaftsarchitekten Burger + Tischer, München.

Der Entwurf aus dem Büro Hilmer & Sattler und Albrecht besticht, so die Jury, »durch die Idee, den Schwung der eiszeitlichen Isarhangkante durch eine Bebauung zu fassen«. Ein weiteres Qualitätsmerkmal erkennt die Jury »im Bezug zwischen Bebauung und Park«, denn der Bavariapark soll zum zentralen Fokus der neuen Bebauung werden und durch die Prägnanz der Baukörper und die dort angeordnete Ringstraße Öffentlichkeit und repräsentativen Charakter erhalten.

Die im sanften Schwung die Hangkante links und rechts von Bavaria und Ruhmeshalle begleitenden langen Blöcke bilden die Matrize für die um den Bavariapark gedachten, U-förmigen Büro- und Wohneinheiten. Für jeden Block sahen die Architekten sechs Stockwerke plus Staffelgeschoß und bastionsartige Ecktürme zum Park hin vor sowie weite Innenhöfe, die öffentliches und privates Grün hervorragend verbinden. Trotz dieser scheinbaren Gleichartigkeit der Blöcke sieht die Jury den Gedanken der Vielfalt eingeschrieben, wenn sie unterstellt, »daß die Blockrandbebauung auch kleinteilig in Einzelgebäuden erfolgen kann«. Ein solches Herangehen – wenn auch in anderem Maßstab – funktioniert, das haben Hilmer & Sattler bereits mit ihren beiden Wohnhäusern auf der »documenta urbana« (1979–82) in Kassel-Dönche bewiesen. Diese reihen sich gemeinsam mit den unterschiedlich ausgeformten, viergeschossigen Wohnbauten der anderen beteiligten Architekten (u. a. Otto Steidle) in einer schlangenartigen Zeilenfigur aneinander und bilden in ihrer Vielfalt doch erkennbar einen Baukörper.

Das Büro Ortner & Ortner fühlt sich ebenso wie Otto Steidle und Hilmer & Sattler und Albrecht dem städtebaulichen Leitbild der europäischen Stadt verpflichtet und versucht, dies in seinen Entwurf mit einer stringenten Blockstruktur auf das Gelände der Theresienhöhe zu übertragen. Ortner & Ortner lassen in ihrem *Wörterbuch der Baukunst* notieren, daß der städtische Block, also die Gesamtheit mehrerer Häuser, die Kraft hat, den von der Moderne zersprengten und unerkennbar gemachten Stadtkörper wieder zurückzugewinnen. Ähnlich wie Hilmer & Sattler und Albrecht schließen sie die Blöcke nicht, sondern öffnen sie sowohl zum Bavariapark wie auch zur Ganghoferstraße hin. So entstehen durchlässige Blöcke, die zur Straße Büros und zum Park Wohnnutzung beherbergen sollen.

Die Jury lobte vor allem die Ausarbeitung des öffentlichen Raumes mit dem gestuften System qualifizierter und differenzierter Freiräume und deren gelungene Vernetzung: »Durch die Platzabfolge über den belassenen Georg-Freundorfer-Platz, den Marktplatz, den Museumsplatz, den Quartiersplatz sowie kleinen städtischen Aufweitungen und Achsen wird eine Verknüpfung der Stadtquartiere bis zum Westpark hin erreicht und eine spannungsvolle Hierarchie der Grünflächen hergestellt.«

Wohnen am Bavariapark

Wir gehen vorbei an dem urbanen Riegel der Kontorhäuser und begeben uns ins Herz der Anlage, die zum Park hin immer durchlässiger zu werden scheint. Es wird gewohnt, und es wird deutlich, was Otto Steidle meint, wenn er sagt: »Das Haus dient dem Raum.« Die acht Wohnhäuser staffeln sich in der Tiefe zum Park hin, Räume entstehen, in die das Grün des Bavariaparks hineinwirkt, Durchblicke tun sich auf. Hier ist Steidle das Paradox gelungen, eine innerstädtische Siedlung ohne Siedlungscharakter entwickelt zu haben, die hochverdichtet ist und dabei den Eindruck von Weite nicht vermissen läßt.

Das unsichtbare Bindeglied der Gesamtanlage ist die zweigeschossige Tiefgarage, geplant von Steidle + Partner, die den Komplex inklusive der Kontorhäuser unterzieht und das Gebiet von störenden Parkplätzen freihält. Hier begann die aktive Zusammenarbeit der drei Architekturbüros. Man traf sich in wöchentlichen Planungssitzungen, um sich miteinander abzustimmen und Probleme einvernehmlich auszuräumen. Zu dieser Zusammenarbeit kam es, weil die in den Kaufverträgen der Grundstücke festgeschriebene Durchführung von Wettbewerben mit einer Ausnahme versehen wurde. Die Qualität der Planung könne auch bei einer Direktbeauftragung mehrerer herausragender Teilnehmer des städtebaulichen Ideenwettbewerbs gewahrt bleiben.

Ein 60 cm hoher Sockel erhebt die Wohnanlage leicht über das umliegende Terrain und zieht sie zu einem Ganzen zusammen. Im Vertrauen des Architekten in die Wirkung symbolischer Schwellen sollte dieser Unterbau ursprünglich die einzige Abtrennung vom öffentlichen Raum markieren. Doch das war sowohl dem Bauherrn wie wohl auch den Eigentümern nicht nur in Anbetracht der zu erwartenden Besucherströme des Verkehrsmuseums und der herbstlichen Wiesnhorden zu wenig. Schließlich sollen die vom Autoverkehr freigehaltenen Straßen gerade auch die angestammten Bewohner des Westends einladen, den wieder zugänglichen alten Messepark in Besitz zu nehmen. Bei den Nutzern des südlich benachbarten Jugendzentrums in der Alten Feuerwache am neu benannten Sinti-Roma-Platz ist man sich auch nicht sicher, ob sie die Hierar-

9. Theodor Fischer, Ledigenheim, München, 1927. (Photo: Klaus Kinold.)
10. Steidle+Partner, Am Bavariapark. Ideenskizze von Otto Steidle.

9. Theodor Fischer, Ledigenheim (home for singles), Munich, 1927. (Photo: Klaus Kinold.)
10. Steidle+Partner, Am Bavariapark. Concept sketch by Otto Steidle.

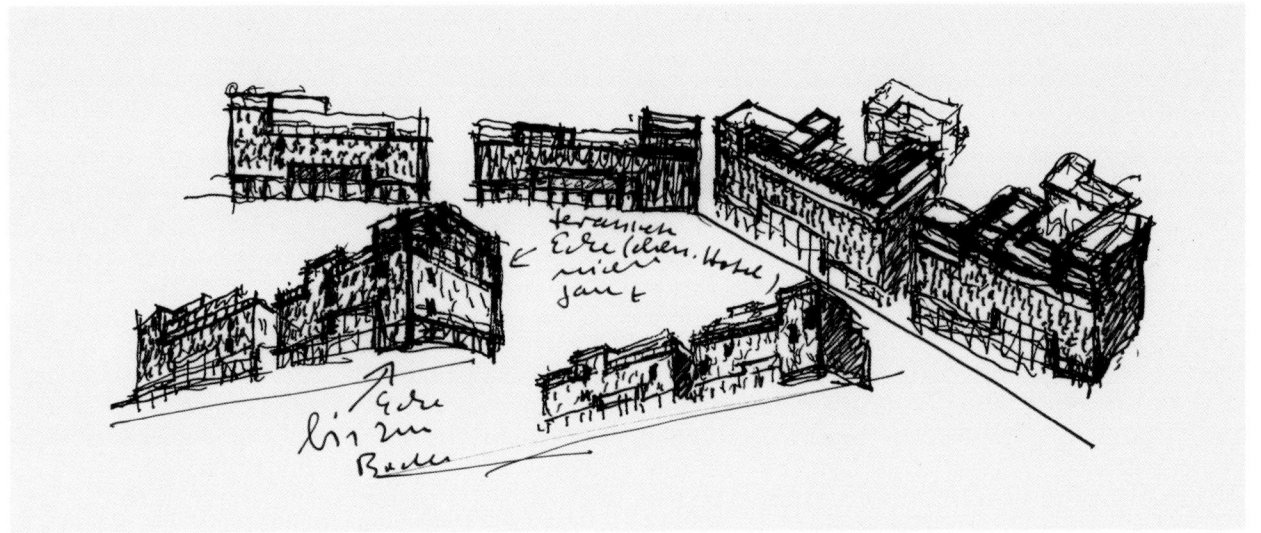

the Bavariapark is intended to become a central focal point of the new development and acquire public quality and prestigious character from the succinct nature of the buildings and the ring road placed there.

The long blocks accompanying the development in a gentle curve on the edge of the slope to the left and right of the Bavariapark and Hall of Fame form a matrix for the office and housing units that were to be placed in a U-shape around the Bavariapark. The architects intended each block to have six storeys plus a staggered storey, with bastion-like towers on the park side and wide inner courtyards, wonderfully linking public and private green spaces. Despite the fact that the blocks all seemed to be alike, the jury sees that the idea of diversity is built in when they assume »that the block periphery development can also take place on a small scale in the individual buildings.« Hilmer & Sattler have already proved that an approach of this kind can work – though on a different scale – with their two apartment blocks for »documenta urbana« (1979–82) in Dönche, Kassel. Along with the variously shaped, four-storey apartment blocks by the other participating architects (including Otto Steidle), the Hilmer & Sattler buildings follow a snaking line, but clearly form a single entity despite their diversity.

Like Otto Steidle and Hilmer & Sattler und Albrecht, Ortner & Ortner also felt a clear commitment to the European city as an urban guideline, and tried to transfer this to the Theresienhöhe site with a compelling block structure in their design. In their dictionary of architecture, Ortner & Ortner note that the urban block, in other words a number of buildings forming a unit, has the power to bring the city back to life as a body, after it had been blown to pieces and made unrecognizable by Modernism. Similarly to Hilmer & Sattler und Albrecht, they do not close the blocks, but open them up to Ganghoferstraße and the Bavariapark. This creates permeable blocks, intended for offices on the street side and housing facing the park.

The jury praised the development of the public space in particular, with its graduated system of qualified and differentiated open space, successfully linked together: »The urban quarters are linked together right up to the Westpark by the sequence of squares via Georg-Freundorfer-Platz, which is left as it is, the market, museum and district squares, and also small urban widenings and axes, creating a tensioned hierarchy of green spaces.«

Living by the Bavariapark

We walk past the urban line of office blocks and on to the heart of the complex, which seems to become increasingly permeable the closer we get to the park. People are living there, and we begin to see what Otto Steidle means when he says: »The building serves the space.« The eight apartment blocks are staggered further and further back towards the park, creating spaces into which the green of the Bavariapark penetrates, views begin to open up. Here Steidle has paradoxically managed to develop an inner-city housing estate that does not seem like an estate, high in density and yet making sure that there is still an impressive of breadth.

The invisible link within the complex as a whole is the two-storey underground car park, planned by Steidle + Partner. This runs under the whole complex including the office buildings and keeps the area free of irritating surface parking. This is where the three architectural practices started to work together. Weekly planning meetings were held to reach agreements and solve problems jointly. This co-operation arose because an exception was made to the competition conditions laid down in the land purchase agreements: if several outstanding participants in the urban development competition were commissioned directly, planning quality could still be maintained.

A 60 cm high base raises the housing complex slightly above the surrounding terrain and pulls it together into a whole. The architect's confidence in the effectiveness of invisible thresholds meant that this substructure was originally intended to mark the only separation from the public space. But this was not enough for the clients or the owners, given the numbers of visitors the transport museum was expecting and the hordes attending the Oktoberfest. Ultimately the streets, kept free of car traffic, are also intended to tempt the established Westend residents to take possession of the old exhibition centre park, which is now accessible again. It is also still not certain whether the users of the youth centre adjacent to the south in the Old Fire Station in the rechristened Sinti-Roma-Platz will respect the hierarchy of public, semi-public and private open spaces. And so now there is a fence to surmount if people want to get closer to the buildings.

Steidle used a planning trick to bind the two office blocks into the residential development. Their two

chie von öffentlichen, halböffentlichen und privaten Freiflächen respektieren werden. Und so bildet heute ein Zaun die Hürde, die es zu überwinden gilt, will man sich den Häusern nähern.

Durch einen planerischen Trick gelang es Steidle, die beiden Kontorhäuser in die Wohnbebauung einzugliedern. Ihre beiden »Querriegel«, die den Blockrand nach innen zu einem großen »F« werden lassen, bilden zugleich die erste von drei Reihen auf einem Schachbrett mit acht weiteren Mitspielern. Sie weisen den anderen ihren Standort auf dem Feld zu und geben ihnen das Bauvolumen vor. Der ruhige Wechsel der Fensterbreiten wird auf der Parkseite weitergeführt, jedoch ersetzte Steidle die großstädtische Mischung aus repräsentativen Materialien und gedeckter Farbigkeit durch Putzfassaden in kräftigen Farben. Dadurch verschwimmen die Grenzen von Büro- und Wohnnutzung; auf den ersten Blick soll hier nicht erkennbar sein, was hinter den Fassaden passiert.

Alleiniges Erkennungsmerkmal des Wohnens: Die Häuser stehen frei. Sie sind allseitig durchfenstert und haben zum Teil weit auskragende Balkone. Der Typus der Stadtvilla stand Pate und wird auch stilistisch bedient. Farbe prägt das Bild, und die jeweilige Handschrift der Architekten zeigt Zusammenhänge auf. Und so sind die insgesamt vier Häuser, je zwei im Rücken der Kontorhäuser Nord und Süd, von Ortner & Ortner ebenso einfach als von einer Hand errichtet zu erkennen wie die drei – zwei auf dem mittleren, eines auf dem südlichen Baufeld – von Hilmer & Sattler und Albrecht. Die Fassade des Steidle-Wohnhauses braucht keinen zweiten Blick, um in ihr die Fortsetzung der Kontorhäuser zu erkennen.

Sehnsucht nach Italien

»Unsere Gebäude«, heißt es bei Ortner & Ortner, »nehmen das Thema einer italienischen Villa auf; sie wird überhöht, sozusagen gestapelt und je nach Lage etwas variiert, bleibt aber doch typisch. Sockel, Schaft und Gesims werden ebenso aufgenommen wie Fensterlaschen und Strukturierung durch Putzfugen. Die Farbgebung – venezianisches Rot, Ocker und Steingrau – versucht das Thema auf den Punkt zu bringen: ein Stück italienischer Sehnsucht – im Alltagsformat – auf der Theresienhöhe.«

Zentral erschlossen, befinden sich drei unterschiedlich große Wohnungen auf jedem Alltags- oder Regelgeschoß der vier Wohnbauten. Einige Wohnungen sind als Maisonnettes ausgeführt, jede verfügt über einen Balkon oder eine von zwei Seiten belichtete Loggia. Bis auf die Küchen- und Badezimmerfenster sind alle Wandöffnungen als raumhohe, zweiflügelige französische Fenstertüren ausgebildet und mit einem einfachen, dunklen Stahlgeländer versehen. Die Wohnungsgrößen sind familientauglich, ihre Ausstattung ist, mit zum Teil zwei Bädern, hoch.

Die jeweiligen Dachgeschosse werden der Bezeichnung Villa noch am ehesten gerecht. Hier teilen sich maximal zwei Wohnungen die Grundfläche des Hauses, und die tiefen Einschnitte in der Kubatur des Blocks markieren dem Grundriß angemessene Dachterrassen.

Dominiert wird das Bild der Wohnbauten von den kräftigen weißen Balkon- und Loggiagittern, den hochrechteckigen, ebenfalls weißen Fenstern und den mal breiten, mal etwas schmaleren dazwischenliegenden farbigen Wandflächen. Zusammen mit den auskragenden Kranzgesimsen entsteht der Eindruck einfacher, aber tiefer, plastischer Fassaden, die Ruhe und eine gewisse Vertikalität ausstrahlen. Die Fassadenfeinheiten werden erst bei genauer Betrachtung offenbar: Das leichte Verrücken aller Fenster der ersten Obergeschosse aus der Achse birgt eine eigentümliche Spannung und trägt dazu bei, den bereits farblich abgesetzten Sockel noch deutlicher von den Hauptgeschossen zu trennen. Die zwischen dem 2. und 6. Obergeschoß verbundenen weißen Laschen der Loggien ziehen die fünf Hauptgeschosse optisch zusammen, während die tiefen Einschnitte ins oberste Geschoß den Bauten eine gewisse Leichtigkeit geben, die im wohlakzentuierten Kontrast zur Strenge des auskragenden Kranzgesimses steht.

Mit den großen Balkonen, die sich geradezu nach der Sonne recken, den breiten Fenstertüren und ihrer Farbigkeit stehen die Häuser so selbstverständlich für »Wohnen« und »Italien«, daß es eigentlich keiner weiteren Erklärung bedarf. Denn das Erklären kennzeichnet nach dem Ortnerschen *Wörterbuch der Baukunst* »eine Zwangslage, die aus der Unsicherheit des Architekten resultiert, was er an Wissen, an Bescheidwissen voraussetzen darf«. Wohnen versteht hier jeder sofort, und auch die Anspielungen an Italien sind leicht ablesbar, die Bilder, die einem in den Sinn kommen, vielfältig. Daß sie zuerst wenig mit Farbe zu tun haben, liegt am Schwarzweiß des italienischen Kinos der fünfziger und sechziger Jahre: Anna Magnani als Mama Roma in einem dieser typischen Vororte Roms. Verwehte Bushaltestellen, dahinter die sich abzeichnende Silhouette der schlanken Wohnhäuser, belebte Balkone, Dachüberstände. Farbig werden die Bilder erst in der Erinnerung an die Vorstädte Genuas, an gleißendes Licht und Sonnenbaden auf der Dachterrasse mit grandiosem Blick auf das Mittelmeer. Daß bei den vier »Alltagsvillen« von Ortner & Ortner die Farbe Rot vorherrscht, ist nicht nur italienischen Vorbildern geschuldet, denn Rot erscheint, anders als Blau, lebhaft und freundlich, so ihre Definition im *Wörterbuch*. »Die Röte des Rots hat viele verschiedene Namen: Es gibt ein pompejanisches Rot, ein Tizian-Rot, ein Siena-Rot ... Allen gemeinsam ist die pulsierende Kraft des Lebendigen.«

Feinplastische Fassadengliederung

Die drei Wohnhäuser von Hilmer & Sattler und Albrecht reihen sich in eine Gruppe von Wohnbauten ein, die das Büro in den letzten Jahren entworfen hat und die trotz aller Unterschiede von Ausstattung und Größe doch formale Ähnlichkeiten aufweist. Die etwa gleichzeitig mit der Theresienhöhe entwickelte Wohnbebauung am Olympiaberg in München verwendet ebenso wie die beiden 1997 bis 2000 realisierten Wohnhäuser am Klingelhöfer-Dreieck in Berlin einen dreiteiligen Fassadenaufriß, das Motiv loggienartiger Balkone, stehende Fensterformate und eine zurückhaltende Farbigkeit. Eine gewisse Ambivalenz zwischen traditioneller Architektur und Moderne will das Gestaltungsprinzip der Fassaden bei allen drei Standorten wohl bewußt aufbauen, jedoch sind die Bauten der Theresienhöhe mit sieben und acht Geschossen höher und wirken auf diese Weise vielleicht etwas städtischer als die beiden anderen, wenn auch die urbane Dichte bei allen etwa gleich hoch ist.

11. Hilmer & Sattler und Albrecht, Haus 4. Skizze von Christoph Sattler.
12. Steidle+Partner, Haus 6. Skizze von Otto Steidle.

transverse bars, which make the inside block periphery into a large »F«, also form the first of three rows on a chessboard with eight other players. They indicate where the others should be in the pattern and prescribe the volume for their buildings. The calmly changing window widths continue on the park side, but Steidle replaced the metropolitan mixture of prestigious materials and subdued colouring with rendered façades in strong colours. This blurs the boundaries between office and residential use; it should not be possible to work out what is happening behind the façades at a first glance.

The only clear sign that buildings are to be lived in: they are free-standing. They have continuous windows on all sides and some have widely protruding balconies. The urban villa provided the idea, and is used stylistically as well. Colour shapes the image, and different architects' handwriting makes connections. And so the total of four buildings, two each behind the two office blocks, by Ortner & Ortner, are just as clearly designed by the same hand as the three – two on the centre building area, one on the southern plot – by Hilmer & Sattler und Albrecht. And it does not take a second look at the façade of the Steidle apartment block to recognize it as a continuation of the office buildings.

Longing for Italy

»Our buildings«, say Ortner & Ortner, »take up the theme of an Italian villa; it is made higher, piled up, so to speak, and varied to an extent according to position, but it remains typical. Base, shaft and cornice are taken up, and so are the window flaps and structuring using rendered joints. The colour scheme – Venetian red ochre and stone grey – tries to sum up the theme: a piece of longing for Italy – in an everyday format – on the Theresienhöhe.«

There are three dwellings of different sizes, with central access, on each of the ordinary or regular floors of the four apartment blocks. Some of the dwellings are maisonettes, but each has a balcony or a loggia lit from two sides. With the exception of the kitchen and bathroom windows, all the wall apertures are in the form of room-high, two-leaved french windows, with a simple steel handrail. The dwellings are of a suitable size for families, some with the relatively lavish provision of two bathrooms.

But it is the top floors that best fit in with the term villa. Here a maximum of two dwellings share the area of the full building, and the deep incisions into the cubature of the block mark roof terraces appropriate to the ground plan.

The picture is dominated by powerful white balcony and loggia grilles, the vertically rectangular windows, also white and the coloured wall areas in between, sometimes wide and sometimes narrower. These and the protruding cornices give the impression of simple but deep three-dimensional façades, emanating calm and a certain vertical quality. Closer examination is needed to discover the refinements in the façade: all the windows in the first floors are shifted slightly off the axis; this conceals a strange tension and helps to divided the bases, which are already separated in terms of colour, even more clearly from the main floors. The white flaps on the loggias, linked between the 2nd and 6th floors, pull the five main floors together visually, while the deep incisions into the top floor give the buildings a certain lightness, which forms a well-accented contrast with the austerity of the protruding cornice.

With their large balconies, almost reaching out towards the sun, wide, tall windows and sense of colour, these buildings say »dwellings« and »Italy« so clearly that no further explanation is actually needed. In fact, according the Ortner's dictionary of architecture, explaining is »a predicament resulting from the architect's uncertainty about what he can assume in terms of knowledge, of certain knowledge«. Here everyone will think immediately that these are buildings to be lived in, and the allusions to Italy are readily understood as well, and a very wide range of images is invoked. The fact that they have very little to do with colour in the first place is because of the black-and-white world of Italian films in the nineteen-fifties and -sixties: Anna Magnani as Mama Roma in one of those typical Roman suburbs. Bleak bus-stops, behind them the emerging silhouettes of the slender apartment blocks, lively balconies, overhanging roofs. Colour does not come into the images until we remember the suburbs of Genoa, blinding light and sunbathing on the roof terrace with a wonderful view of the Mediterranean. The fact that the colour red is dominant in Ortner & Ortner's four »everyday« villas is not just due to Italian models. Red, unlike blue, seems lively and friendly, according to its definition in the dictionary. »The redness of red goes by many different names: there is Pompeian red, Titian red, Sienna red ... All share the pulsating power of the living.«

Refined three-dimensional façade articulation

The three apartment blocks by Hilmer & Sattler und Albrecht fit in with a group of residential buildings designed by the practice in recent years, showing formal similarities despite all the differences in size and finish. The residential development on the Olympiaberg in Munich, developed about the same time as the Theresienhöhe project, like the two apartment blocks realized at the Klingelhöfer Triangle in Berlin from 1997 to 2000, use a three-part façade elevation, the loggia-like balcony motif, vertical window formats and a reticent colour scheme. Probably the design principle behind the façades for all three locations is deliberately trying to create a certain ambivalence between traditional architecture and Modernism, but the Theresienhöhe buildings are taller, with seven and eight storeys, and hence perhaps seem somewhat more urban than the other two, even though the urban density is about the same in all cases.

For Hilmer & Sattler und Albrecht, the fact that the buildings are free-standing created the central element of quality, in this case resulting from Otto Steidle's master plan, as the windows facing in all directions make for the best possible lighting, and also provide more scope in terms of ground plan design. And so each of these dwellings opens out in at least three directions, and the 2-bedroom flats even have windows on three sides. The impression of general openness is further underlined by the room-high vertical windows, the widely protruding balconies and the large roof terraces, and the colour adds to this impression as well.

Das Freistellen der Gebäude auf der Theresienhöhe stellt für Hilmer & Sattler und Albrecht die zentrale, hier aus dem Masterplan Otto Steidles resultierende Qualität dar, da es durch Rundumbefensterung nach allen Himmelsrichtungen optimale Belichtungsmöglichkeiten und auch, was die Grundrißgestaltung anbelangt, größere Freiräume zuläßt. Und so öffnet sich jede ihrer Wohnungen nach mindestens zwei Himmelsrichtungen, die 3-Zimmer-Wohnungen sogar nach drei. Der Eindruck der allseitigen Öffnung wird durch die raumhohen Fenstertüren, die weit auskragenden Balkone und die großen Dachterrassen noch unterstrichen, und auch die Farbe trägt zu diesem Eindruck bei.

Die drei Häuser unterscheiden sich durch zwei Merkmale: Zwei werden von den Architekten als »scharfkantig« bezeichnet und eines als »organisch geschwungen«. Bei den scharfkantigen Häusern bilden je vier spiegelsymmetrisch angeordnete 2-Zimmer-Wohnungen, jede mit einem Balkon versehen, die Regelgeschosse, während hinter der geschwungenen Fassade das Regelschoß aus zwei 3-Zimmer- und einer 2-Zimmer-Wohnung, auch jeweils mit Balkon, besteht. Auch Hilmer & Sattler und Albrecht lassen den Alltag im 6. Obergeschoß ausklingen und wenden sich im Dachgeschoß dem luxuriöseren Wohnen zu: Je eine Wohnung besetzt das ganze Dach, und alle zusammen spielen »das Thema Terrasse in verschiedenen Varianten durch«: schmale offene Terrassen, breite, von einer Art Wolkenbügel gerahmte, überdachte und nicht überdachte Terrassen.

Mit ihren Bauten auf der Theresienhöhe gehen Hilmer & Sattler und Albrecht ein Problem offensiv an, das aus dem heutigen Wohnungsbau in Zeiten der Energie-Einsparverordnung nicht mehr wegzudenken ist: »Die von uns geplanten Wohnhäuser sind Beispiele für feinplastische Fassadengliederungen bei Gebäuden mit thermisch gedämmter Außenhaut«, erläutern sie. Es gelingt ihnen, aus der Not eine Tugend zu machen und mit der ungeliebten Wärmedämmung plastische farbige Gliederungsstrukturen zu schaffen, die wechselnde Licht- und Schattenwirkungen auf den Fassaden erzeugen und den jeweiligen Häusern einen unverwechselbaren Ausdruck verleihen.

So werden beim Haus Ben-Chorin-Straße 1 alle Fassadendetails rechtwinklig und scharfkantig ausgebildet, die Horizontale ist das dominierende Element. In den beiden untersten Geschossen ist die Fassade verputzt, das Erdgeschoß wird zusätzlich durch ein Gesimsband von den darüberliegenden Geschossen abgesetzt. Darüber sind die Fenster durch horizontale Brüstungs- und Sturzbänder miteinander verwoben.

Das Haus Ganghoferstraße 35 bildet in seiner rechtwinkligen Umgebung einen organisch geschwungenen Kontrapunkt. »Während bei diesem Haus alle Horizontalen (Stürze und Fensterbänke) scharfkantig ausgebildet sind, sind die Vertikalen gerundet. Diese Ausrundung wird sichtbar erfahren durch den Schatten, den der Sturz auf die Laibung wirft. Die ansonsten unbeliebte ›Thermohaut‹ hat diese Fassadengestaltung ermöglicht.«

Mohnrot und Indisch Gelb

Der Wohnbau von Otto Steidle unterscheidet sich stilistisch stark von den anderen und ist doch eingebettet in den Kontext, da er die Fassadengestaltung der Kontorhäuser aufnimmt, sie, den geänderten Nutzungen folgend, in der Größe variiert und mit Balkonen garniert. Dieses lebendige Bild wird durch die kräftige Farbigkeit noch unterstützt: Alle vier Flanken sind farblich unterschieden. Eine Seite hat Erich Wiesner mit einem satten Rot (er bezeichnet es als Mohnrot) durchgefärbt, die nächste in einem kräftigen Gelbton (»Indisch Gelb, wissen Sie, da ist nicht so viel Weiß drin wie in dem Gelb, das man in München sonst immer sieht«), wobei die oberen beiden Stockwerke in einem helleren Gelb abgesetzt sind. Die verbleibenden Seiten zeigen in den unteren beiden Geschossen wieder das Mohnrot und sind darüber weiß beziehungsweise hellgelb. Die Farben wirken satt und geben dem Bau etwas Weiches. Im Zusammenspiel mit dem Blau, Weiß, Gelb und Braun der Rückfassaden der Kontorhäuser ergeben sich wohltemperierte und gleichzeitig freundliche helle Freiräume. Die braucht es an dieser Stelle aber auch, denn hier im Innersten des Blocks fehlt doch die Weite des Ausblicks auf den Park.

Wie so oft bei Otto Steidle spielt die Erschließung des Baus eine herausragende Rolle. Eine kleine zweigeschossige Halle trägt ebenso wie die zweifarbig schwarz-weißen Wohnungstüren oder die Wiederaufnahme der Fassadenfarbe im Treppenhaus und seine Belichtung durch ein zwei Geschosse übergreifendes Fenster dieser Funktion Rechnung.

Das Haus birgt eine Vielzahl unterschiedlicher Grundrisse und Wohnungstypen: Auf vier Maisonnette-Wohnungen im Erdgeschoß bzw. im 1. Obergeschoß, die über separate hofseitige Eingänge verfügen, folgen lediglich zwei Regelgeschosse mit vier 2- und 3-Zimmer-Wohnungen. Während im 4. Obergeschoß ein Raum erkerartig aus der Bauflucht verschoben wird, teilen sich im 5. Obergeschoß eine Maisonnette- und drei Etagenwohnungen einen Flur. Das 6. Obergeschoß und das Dachgeschoß sind wieder über Maisonnettes verbunden und halten hier oben Wohnungen für die höheren Ansprüche bereit.

So verschieden die Handschriften der drei Architekturbüros sind, so einheitlich präsentiert sich die Wohnanlage als Ganzes. Der zwischen ihr und dem namensgebenden Bavariapark angelegte, vom Autoverkehr freigehaltene Hans-Dürrmeier-Weg trennt, anders als man vermuten könnte, das Quartier nicht von der denkmalgeschützten Gartenanlage, sondern gibt ihm – im Gegenteil – Halt und betont seine Privatheit.

An der Ostseite des Parks tauchen bereits die ersten Gebäude des südlichen Teils der Neubebauung der Theresienhöhe auf. Deutlich tragen sie nicht nur dieselbe städtebauliche Handschrift, sondern übernehmen auch Details wie die hochformatigen Fenster. Wie es scheint, lernen die Architekten der nachfolgenden Häuser vom »Wohnen am Bavariapark«, so wie Otto Steidle zuvor von Theodor Fischer gelernt hatte. In seinem Masterplan hat er sich an dessen Credo gehalten und es damit an die nächste Generation weitergegeben. Theodor Fischer forderte »die starke Verwurzelung mit der Tradition und gleichzeitig die heiße Bemühung um neue Erkenntnisse, neue lebendige Form, neue Gestaltung«.

Literatur

Der München Atlas. Die Metropole im Spiegel faszinierender Karten, hrsg. von Günter Heinritz, Claus-C. Wiegand und Dorothea Wiktorin, Köln 2003, S. 126 f.

Hilmer & Sattler und Albrecht. Bauten und Projekte/Buildings and Projects, Stuttgart/London 2004.

Otto Steidle, Land Stadt Haus, hrsg. von Winfried Nerdinger, Ausstellungskatalog, Architekturmuseum der Technischen Universität München, 2003, S. 105.

»Otto Steidle im Gespräch mit Dr. Michael Schramm«, Bayerischer Rundfunk, Alpha-Forum, 29. September 2003, Manuskript.

Ortner & Ortner, Wörterbuch der Baukunst, Basel, Berlin, Boston 2001.

Stanislaus von Moos, »Humanistische Brennschärfe. Die Architektur von Hilmer & Sattler«, in: *Hilmer & Sattler. Bauten und Projekte/Buildings and Projects*, Stuttgart/London 2000.

The three buildings have two distinguishing characteristics: the architects define two of them as »sharp-edged« and one as »organically curved«. In the sharp-edged buildings the standard floors are made up of four 1-bedroom flats arranged in mirror image, each with a balcony, while behind the curved façade the standard floor consists of two 2-bedroom and one 1-bedroom flat, again each with a balcony. Hilmer & Sattler und Albrecht also say goodbye to anything ordinary on the 6th floor and turn to more luxurious living: one apartment occupies the entire roof in each case, and together they run »through various variations on the terrace theme«: narrow, open terraces, wide terraces framed by a kind of »Cloud Props«, some roofed and some open.

In their buildings on the Theresienhöhe, Hilmer & Sattler und Albrecht take an attacking approach to a problem that has to be faced in modern residential building in these times of energy saving regulations: »The apartment blocks we planned are examples of refined three-dimensional façade articulation for buildings with a thermally insulated outer skin«, they explain. They have successfully made a virtue of necessity by using unloved heat insulation materials to create three-dimensional, coloured structures that produce changing effects of light and shade on the façades, giving each of the buildings an unmistakably expressive quality.

For example, the building at 1 Ben-Chorin-Straße has façade details that are all rectangular and sharp-edged, the horizontal is the formative element. The façade is rendered on the two bottom floors, and the ground floor is additionally set off from the floors above it by a continuous cornice. Above this the windows are linked by horizontal parapet and lintel bands.

The building at 35 Ganghoferstraße provides an organically curved counterpoint within its rectangular surroundings. »In this building all the horizontals (lintels and window-sills) are sharp-edged, but the verticals are rounded. This rounded quality is perceptible visually as a result of the shadow the lintel casts on the reveal. This façade was made possible by the otherwise unloved ›thermal skin‹«.

Poppy red and Indian yellow

Otto Steidle's apartment block is stylistically very different from the others and yet is firmly fixed within the context, as it takes up the façade design of the office buildings, varying it in size according to the changed use pattern, and garnishing it with balconies. This lively image is further supported by the powerful colour scheme: all four flanks are in different hues. Erich Wiesner coloured one side a rich red (he calls it poppy red), the next one a strong shade of yellow (»Indian yellow, you see, there isn't as much white in it as in the yellow you usually see in Munich otherwise«), though the two top floors are set of in a lighter yellow. The remaining sides have the poppy red again on the two lower floors, and are white and light yellow respectively above that. The colours seem rich and give the building a soft quality. The interplay with the blue, white, yellow and brown of the rear façades of the office buildings produces open spaces that are well-tempered and at the same time friendly. But this is something that is really necessary here, as there is no expansive view of the park from right inside the block at this point.

As so often in Otto Steidle's work, access to the building has an outstanding part to play. This aspect is tackled with a small two-storey hall and also the two-coloured black and white apartment doors or the fact that the façade colour is taken up again in the stair well and lighting comes from a window rising through two storeys.

The building contains a variety of different ground plans and accommodation types: four maisonettes on the ground floor and one on the first floor, all with separate entrances on the courtyard side, are followed by just two standard floors with four 1- and 2-bedroom apartments. On the 4th floor, one room is thrust out of the building line like a bay, then the 5th floor and the top floor again contain linked maisonettes, offering accommodation for the more demanding resident.

The handwriting of these three architectural practices is very varied, but the residential complex presents a unified whole. Hans-Dürrmeier-Weg, a car-free thoroughfare between the housing complex and the Bavariapark, which gives the whole development its name, does not cut the quarter off from the listed parkland, but – on the contrary – gives it a hold and makes it feel more private.

The first buildings in the southern section of the new development on the Theresienhöhe are already appearing on the east side of the park. It is quite clear that they do not just share the same urban handwriting, but also take over details like the tall windows. It seems that the architects of the later buildings have learned from »Living by the Bavariapark«, just as Otto Steidle learned from Theodor Fischer. He stuck to his predecessor's credo for his master plan and thus passed it on to the next generation. Theodor Fischer asked for »strong roots connecting with tradition, and at the same time a fervent effort to find new insights, new living forms, new creative design«.

Bibliography

Der München Atlas. Die Metropole im Spiegel faszinierender Karten, ed. by Günter Heinritz, Claus-C. Wiegand, and Dorothea Wiktorin, Cologne, 2003, pp. 126 f.

Hilmer & Sattler und Albrecht. Bauten und Projekte / Buildings and Projects, Stuttgart/London, 2004.

Otto Steidle, Land Stadt Haus, ed. by Winfried Nerdinger, exhibition catalogue, Architekturmuseum der Technischen Universität München, 2003, p. 105.

»Otto Steidle im Gespräch mit Dr. Michael Schramm«, Bayerischer Rundfunk, Alpha-Forum, 29 September 2003, manuscript.

Ortner & Ortner, Wörterbuch der Baukunst, Basel, Berlin, Boston, 2001.

Stanislaus von Moos, »Humanist focus. The architecture of Hilmer & Sattler«, in: *Hilmer & Sattler. Bauten und Projekte / Buildings and Projects*, Stuttgart/London, 2000.

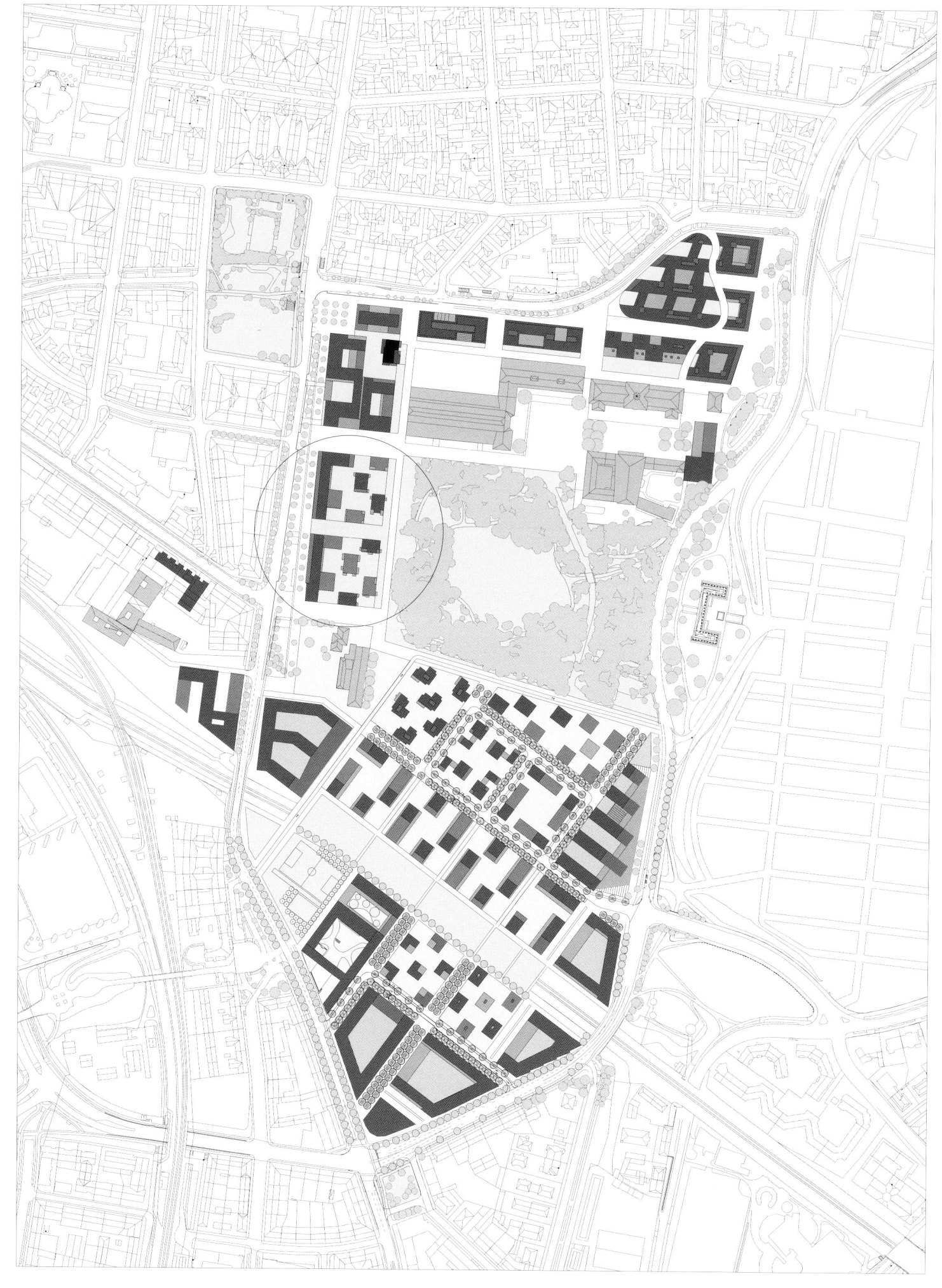

1. Übersichtsplan.
2. Lageplan. Legende: A Steidle+Partner (Kontorhaus Nord), B Steidle+Partner (Kontorhaus Süd), 1 Ortner & Ortner, 2 Ortner & Ortner, 3 Hilmer & Sattler und Albrecht, 4 Hilmer & Sattler und Albrecht, 5 Ortner & Ortner, 6 Steidle+Partner, 7 Ortner & Ortner, 8 Hilmer & Sattler und Albrecht.

1. General plan.
2. Site plan. Key: A Steidle+Partner (north office building), B Steidle+Partner (south office building), 1 Ortner & Ortner, 2 Ortner & Ortner, 3 Hilmer & Sattler und Albrecht, 4 Hilmer & Sattler und Albrecht, 5 Ortner & Ortner, 6 Steidle+Partner, 7 Ortner & Ortner, 8 Hilmer & Sattler und Albrecht.

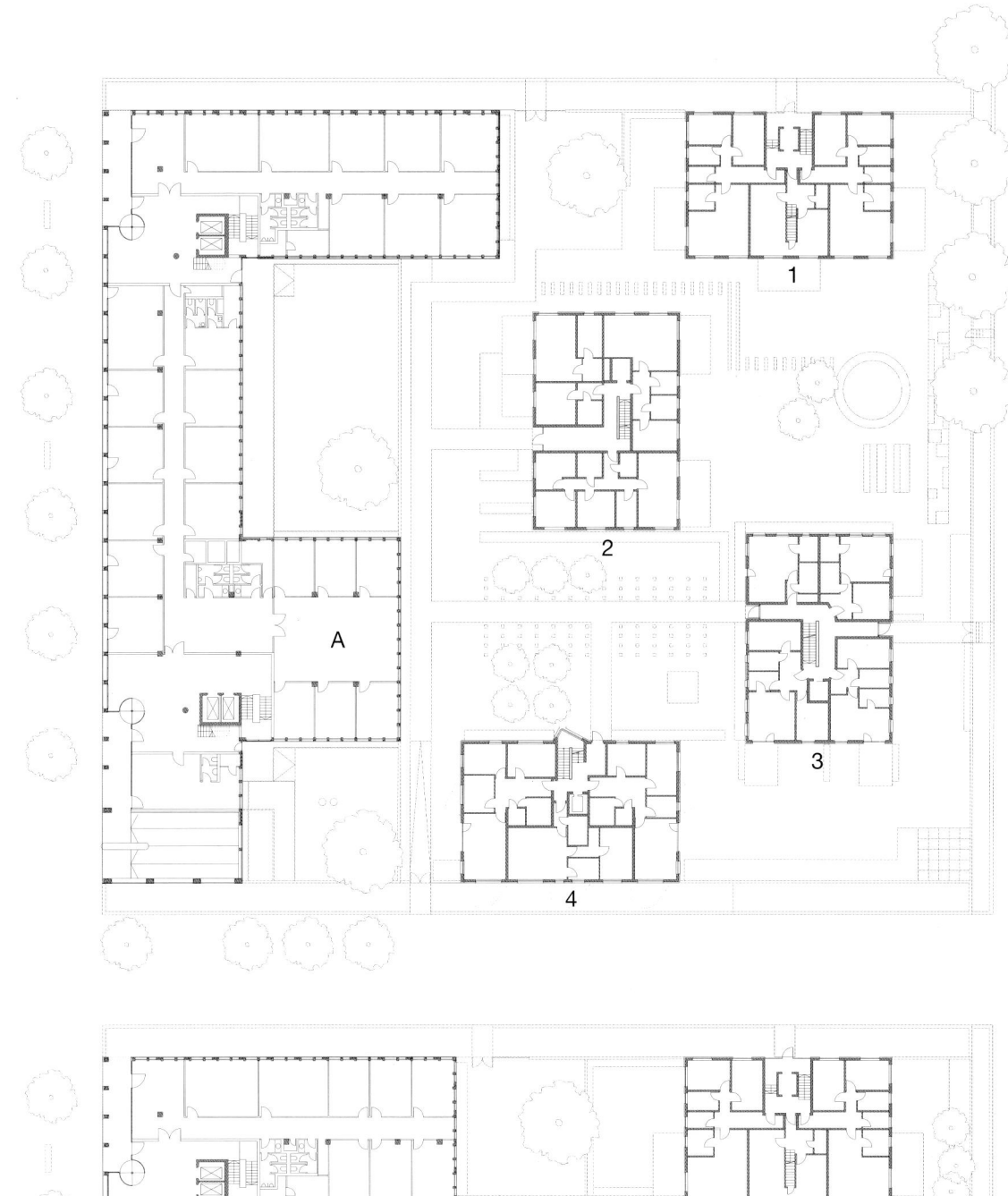

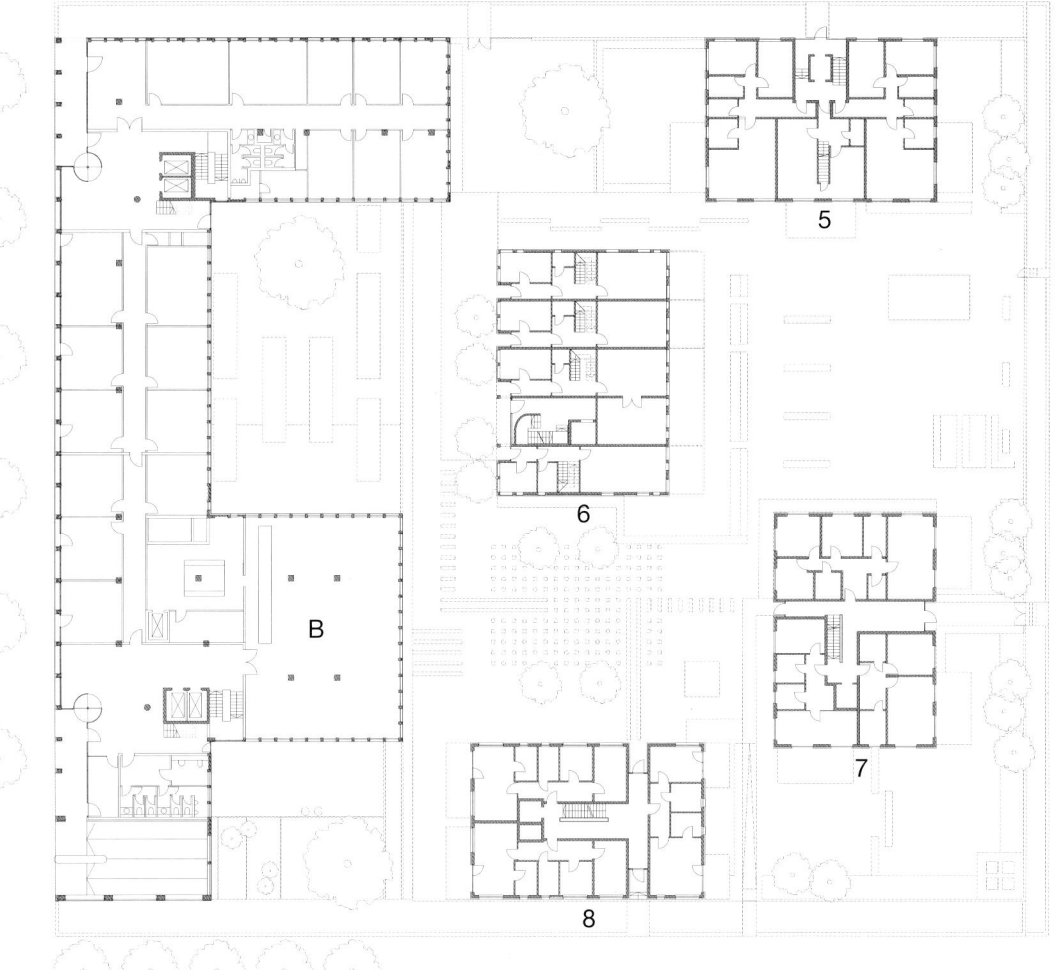

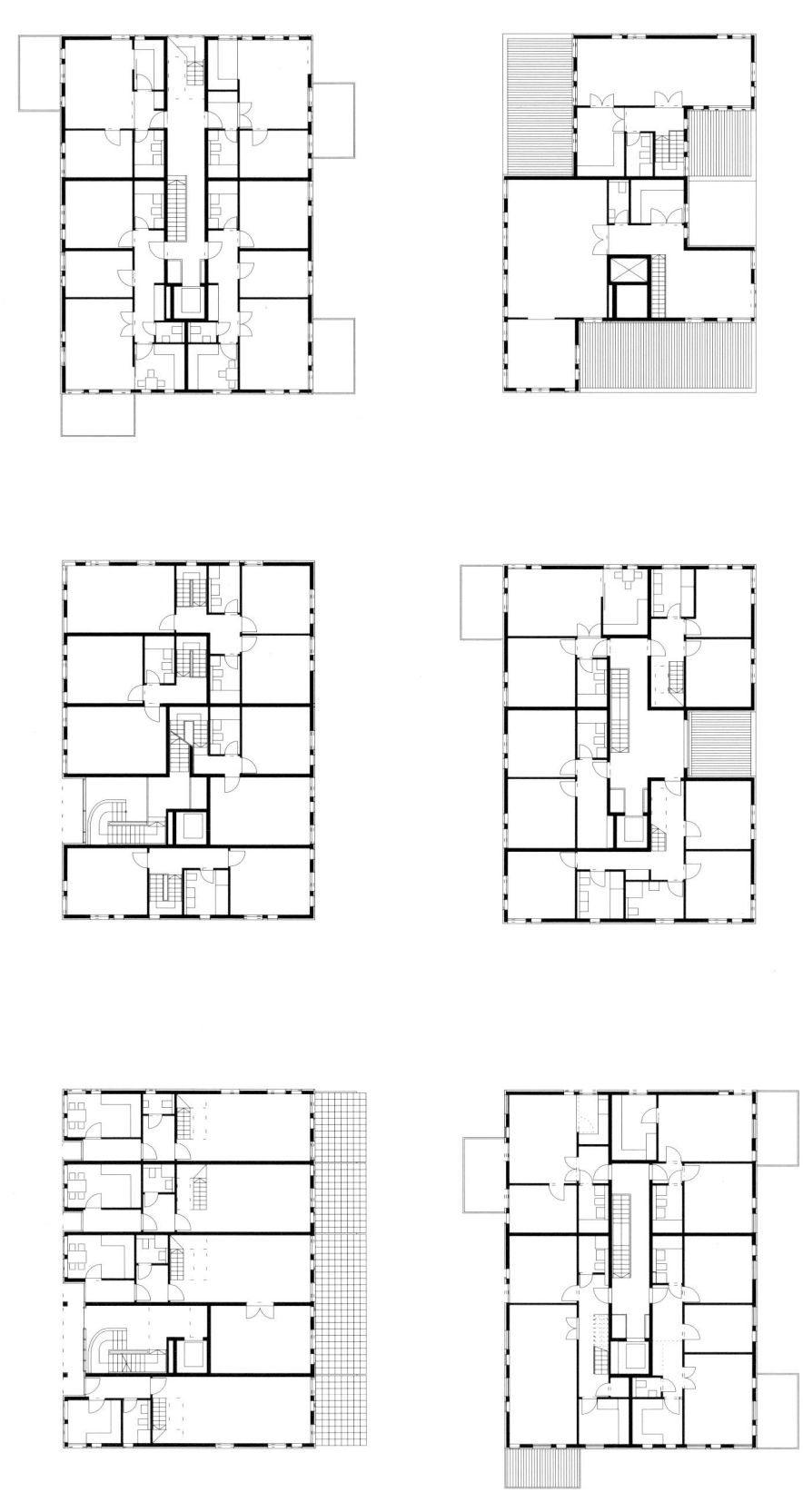
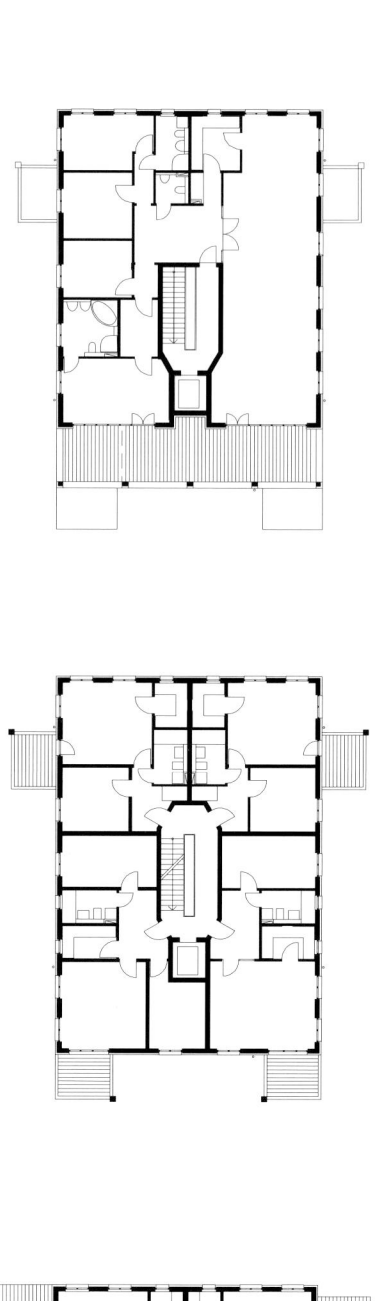
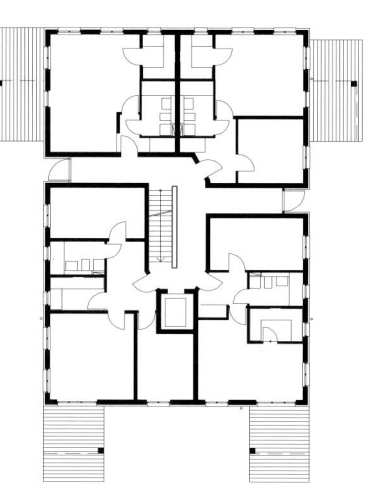

Steidle+Partner (6)

Hilmer & Sattler und Albrecht (3)

3. Steidle + Partner, Haus 6. Grundrisse (Erdgeschoß, 1 Obergeschoß, 2. Obergeschoß, 5. Obergeschoß, 6. Obergeschoß, Dachgeschoß).
4. Hilmer & Sattler und Albrecht, Haus 3. Grundrisse (Erdgeschoß, Regelgeschoß, Dachgeschoß).
5. Hilmer & Sattler und Albrecht, Haus 4. Grundrisse (Erdgeschoß, Regelgeschoß, Dachgeschoß).
6. Ortner & Ortner, Haus 1. Grundrisse (Erdgeschoß, Regelgeschoß, Dachgeschoß).
7. Ortner & Ortner, Haus 7. Grundrisse (Erdgeschoß, Regelgeschoß, Dachgeschoß).

3. Steidle+Partner, house 6. Floor plans (ground floor, 1st floor, 2nd floor, 5th floor, 6th floor, top floor).
4. Hilmer & Sattler und Albrecht, house 3. Floor plans (ground floor, standard floor, top floor).
5. Hilmer & Sattler und Albrecht, house 4. Floor plans (ground floor, standard floor, top floor).
6. Ortner & Ortner, house 1. Floor plans (ground floor, standard floor, top floor).
7. Ortner & Ortner, house 7. Floor plans (ground floor, standard floor, top floor).

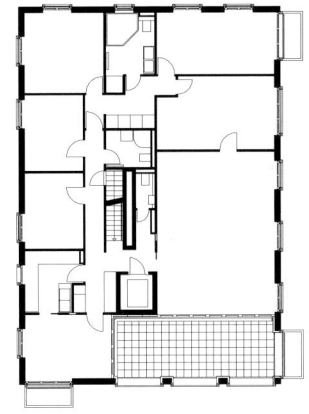
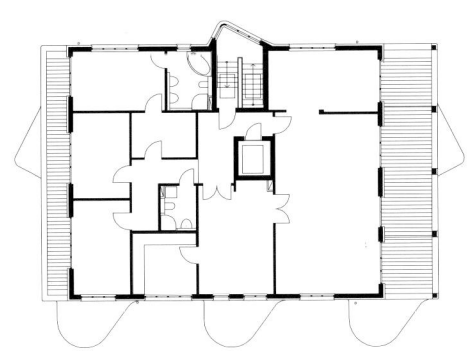

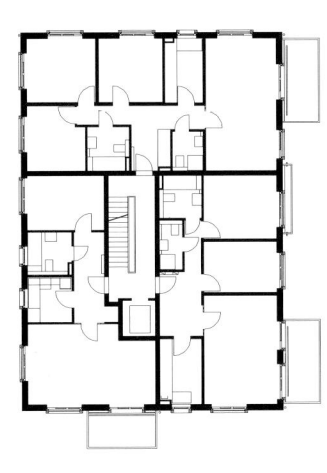
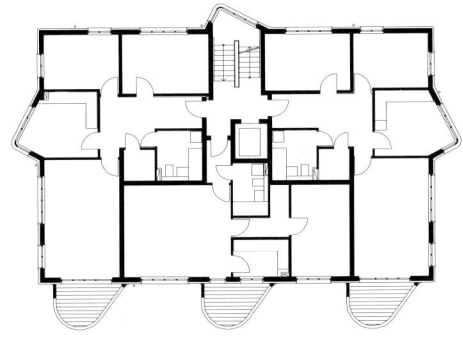
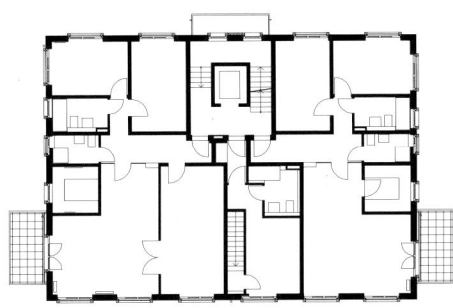
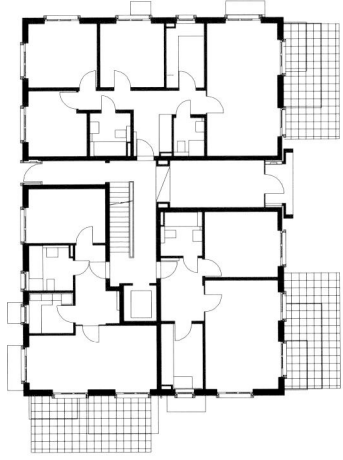
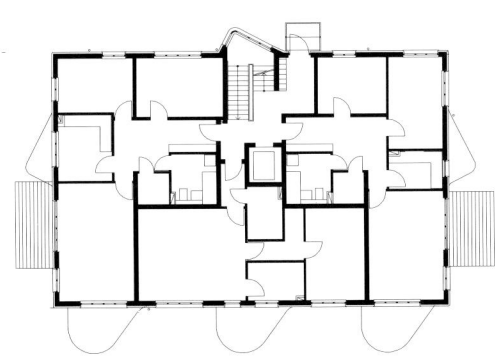
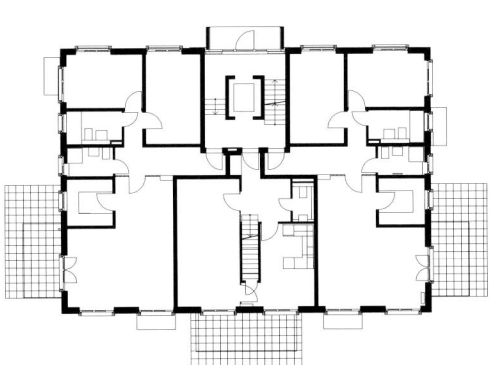

Hilmer & Sattler und Albrecht (4) Ortner & Ortner (1) Ortner & Ortner (7)

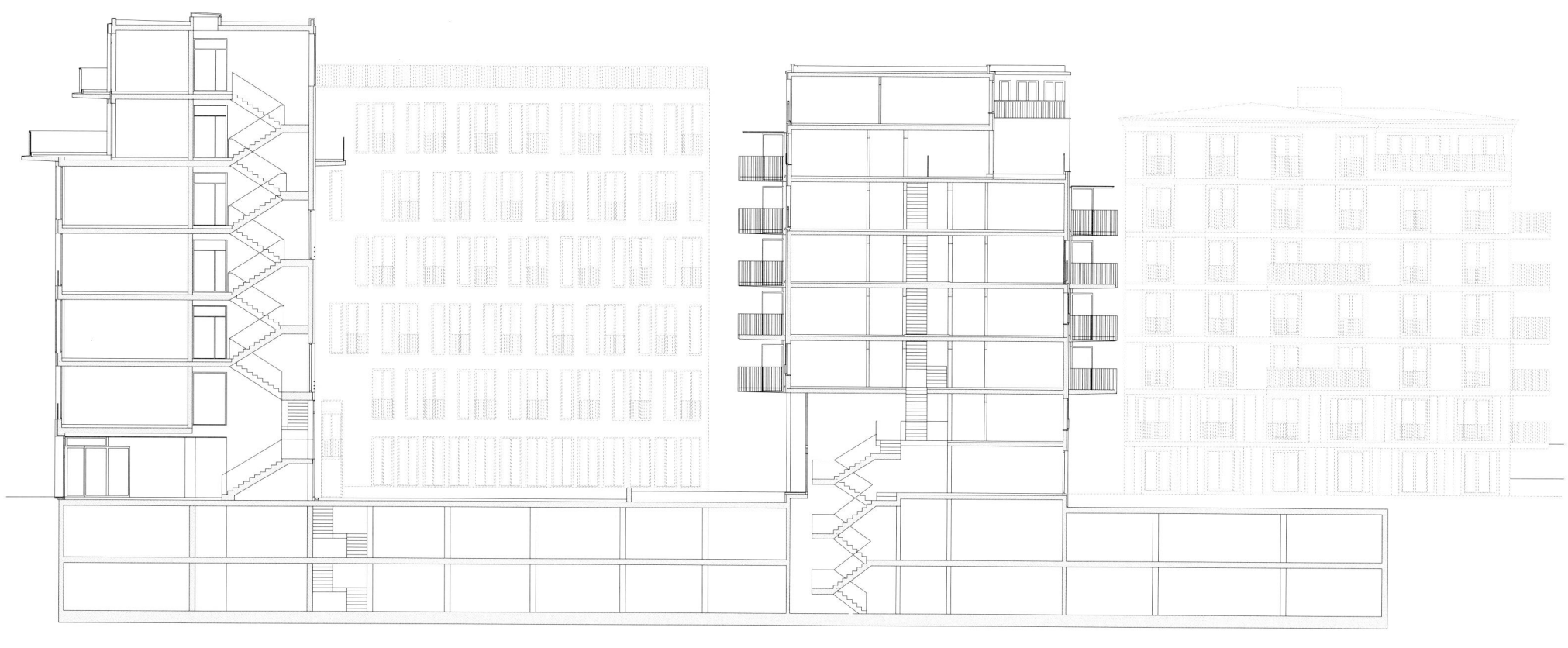

8. Schnitt durch Kontorhaus Süd und Haus 6.
9. Schnitt durch Kontorhaus Süd und Haus 7.

8. Section through south office building and house 6.
9. Section through south office building and house 7.

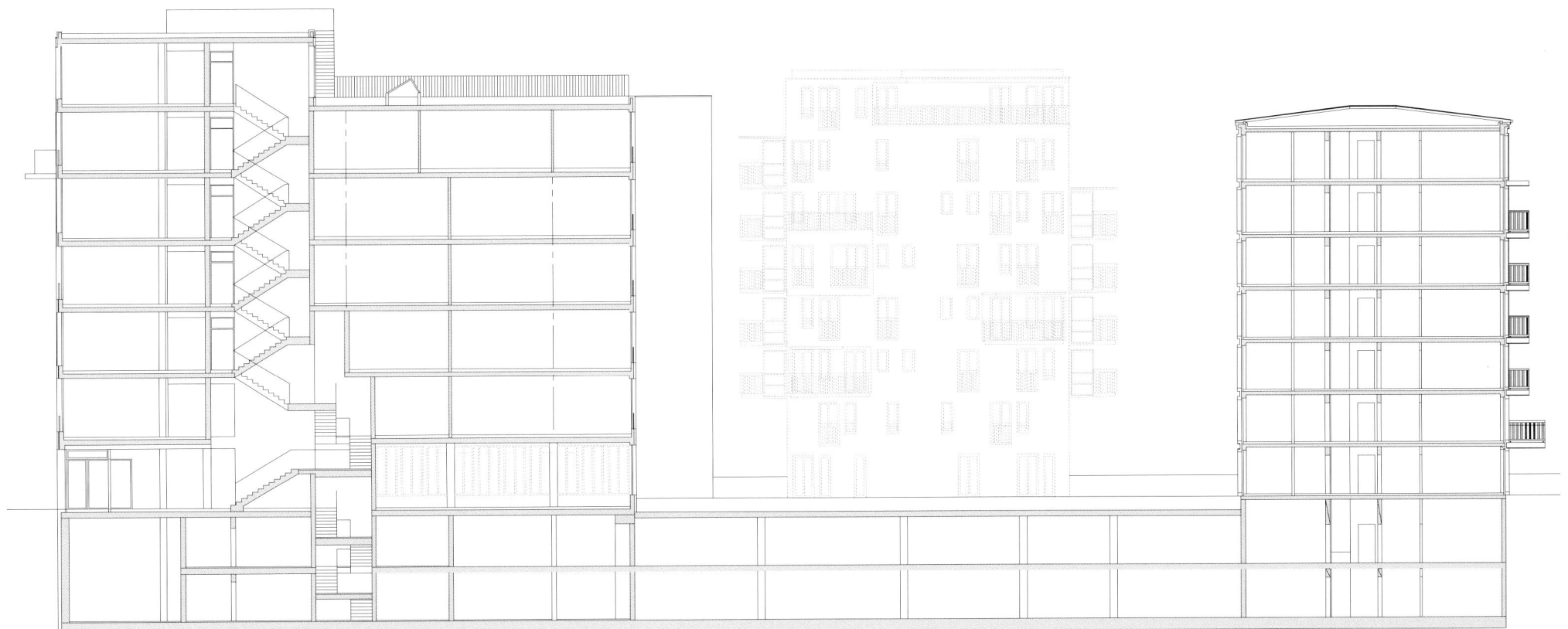

Hilmer & Sattler und Albrecht   Ortner & Ortner   Steidle + Partner   Ortner & Ortner

24

10, 11. Ansicht der Wohnhäuser vom Bavariapark.

10, 11. View of the apartment buildings from the Bavariapark.

Hilmer & Sattler und Albrecht   Hilmer & Sattler und Albrecht   Ortner & Ortner   Ortner & Ortner

S. 26/27
1. Gesamtansicht von Osten. Im Vordergrund der Bavariapark.

p. 26/27
1. General view from the east. The Bavariapark in the foreground.

2. Blick von Osten. Von links nach rechts: Haus 5 (Ortner & Ortner), Haus 4 (Hilmer & Sattler und Albrecht), Haus 3 (Hilmer & Sattler und Albrecht), Haus 2 (Ortner & Ortner).
3. Blick von Osten. Von links nach rechts: Haus 6 (Steidle + Partner), Haus 5 (Ortner & Ortner), Kontorhaus Süd, Haus 4 (Hilmer & Sattler und Albrecht).

2. View from the east. From left to right: house 5 (Ortner & Ortner), house 4 (Hilmer & Sattler und Albrecht), house 3 (Hilmer & Sattler und Albrecht), house 2 (Ortner & Ortner).
3. View from the east. From left to right: house 6 (Steidle + Partner), house 5 (Ortner & Ortner), south office building, house 4 (Hilmer & Sattler und Albrecht).

4. Blick von Südosten. Von links nach rechts: Haus 3 (Hilmer & Sattler und Albrecht), Haus 2 (Ortner & Ortner), Haus 1 (Ortner & Ortner), KPMG-Gebäude.
5. Blick von Südosten. Von links nach rechts: Haus 8 (Hilmer & Sattler und Albrecht), Haus 7 (Ortner & Ortner), Haus 5 (Ortner & Ortner), Haus 3 (Hilmer & Sattler und Albrecht), Haus 1 (Ortner & Ortner).
6. Blick von Osten. Von links nach rechts: Kontorhaus Süd, Haus 4 (Hilmer & Sattler und Albrecht), Haus 3 (Hilmer & Sattler und Albrecht), Haus 2 (Ortner & Ortner).

4. View from the southeast. From left to right: house 3 (Hilmer & Sattler und Albrecht), house 2 (Ortner & Ortner), house 1 (Ortner & Ortner), KPMG building.
5. View from the southeast. From left to right: house 8 (Hilmer & Sattler und Albrecht), house 7 (Ortner & Ortner), house 5 (Ortner & Ortner), house 3 (Hilmer & Sattler und Albrecht), house 1 (Ortner & Ortner).
6. View from the east. From left to right: south office building, house 4 (Hilmer & Sattler und Albrecht), house 3 (Hilmer & Sattler und Albrecht), house 2 (Ortner & Ortner).

7. Blick von Süden. Von links nach rechts: KPMG-Gebäude, Kontorhäuser Nord und Süd.

7. View from the south. From left to right: KPMG building, north and south office buildings.

8. Blick von Süden. Von links nach rechts: Kontorhaus Süd, Haus 6 (Steidle+Partner), Haus 8 (Hilmer & Sattler und Albrecht).
9. Blick von Süden. Von links nach rechts: KPMG-Gebäude, Kontorhäuser Nord und Süd.

8. View from the south. From left to right: south office building, house 6 (Steidle+Partner), house 8 (Hilmer & Sattler und Albrecht).
9. View from the south. From left to right: KPMG building, north and south office buildings.

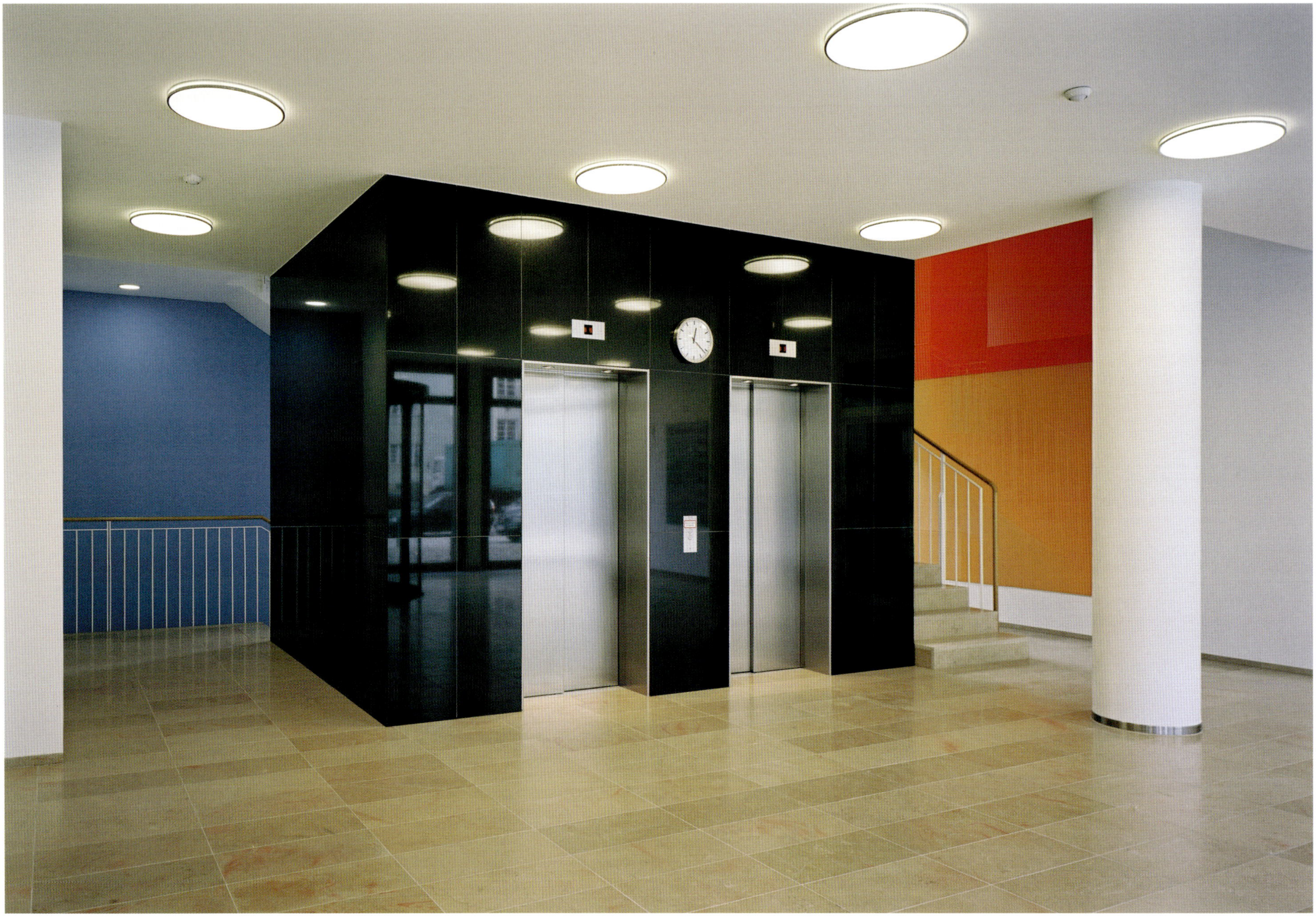

10. Kontorhaus Nord. Eingangshalle.
11. Kontorhaus Süd. Eingangshalle.

10. North office building. Entrance hall.
11. South office building. Entrance hall.

12. Blick von Osten. Von links rechts: Haus 5 (Ortner & Ortner), Haus 6 (Steidle+Partner), Kontorhaus Süd, Haus 4 (Hilmer & Sattler und Albrecht).
13. Blick von Westen. Von links rechts: Kontorhaus Nord, Haus 4 (Hilmer & Sattler und Albrecht), Kontorhaus Süd.

12. View from the east. From left to right: house 5 (Ortner & Ortner), house 6 (Steidle+Partner), south office building, house 4 (Hilmer & Sattler und Albrecht).
13. View from the west. From left to right: north office building, house 4 (Hilmer & Sattler und Albrecht), south office building.

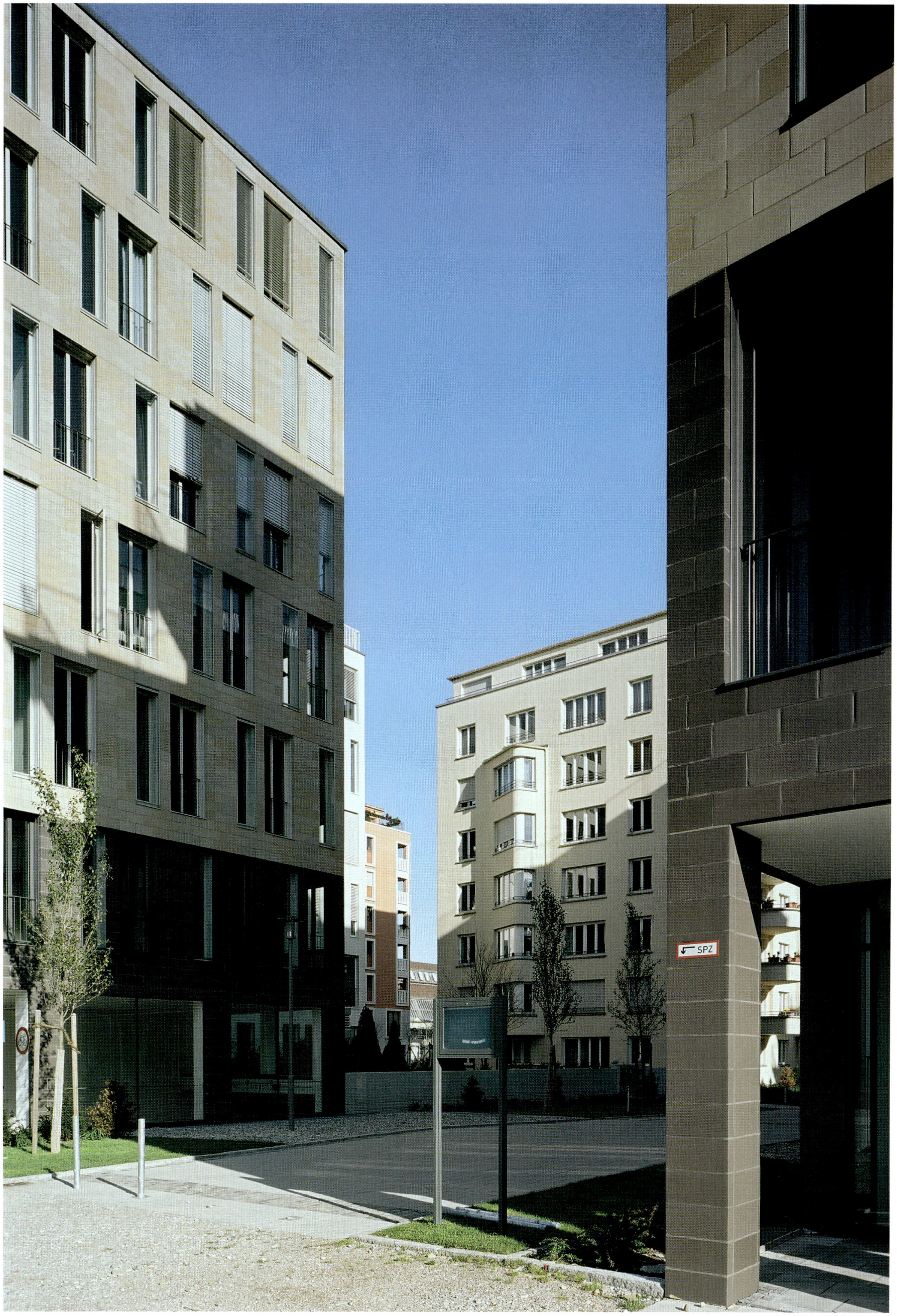
SPZ

14. Blick von Osten. Von links nach rechts: Haus 4 (Hilmer & Sattler und Albrecht), Kontorhaus Nord, Haus 2 (Ortner & Ortner).
15. Blick von Norden. Von links nach rechts: Haus 4 (Hilmer & Sattler und Albrecht), Kontorhaus Süd, Kontorhaus Nord.

14. View from the east. From left to right: house 4 (Hilmer & Sattler und Albrecht), north office building, house 2 (Ortner & Ortner).
15. View from the north. From left to right: house 4 (Hilmer & Sattler und Albrecht), south office building, north office building.

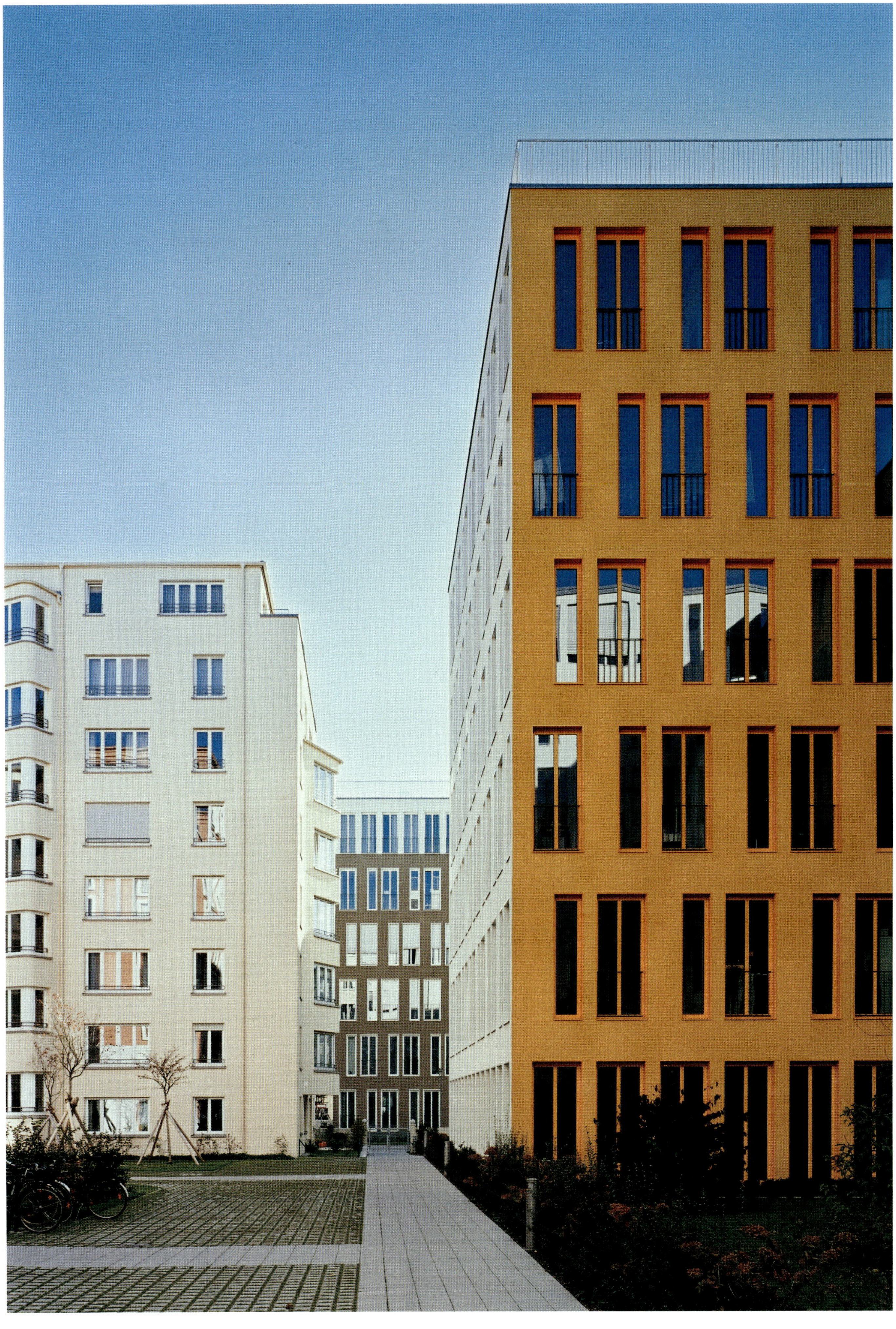

16. Blick von Osten. Von links nach rechts: Haus 7 (Ortner & Ortner), Kontorhaus Süd, Haus 6 (Steidle+Partner), Kontorhaus Nord, Haus 5 (Ortner & Ortner).
17. Blick von Südosten. Von links nach rechts: Kontorhaus Süd, Haus 6 (Steidle+Partner).

16. View from the east. From left to right: house 7 (Ortner & Ortner), south office building, house 6 (Steidle+Partner), north office building, house 5 (Ortner & Ortner).
17. View from the southeast. From left to right: south office building, house 6 (Steidle+Partner).

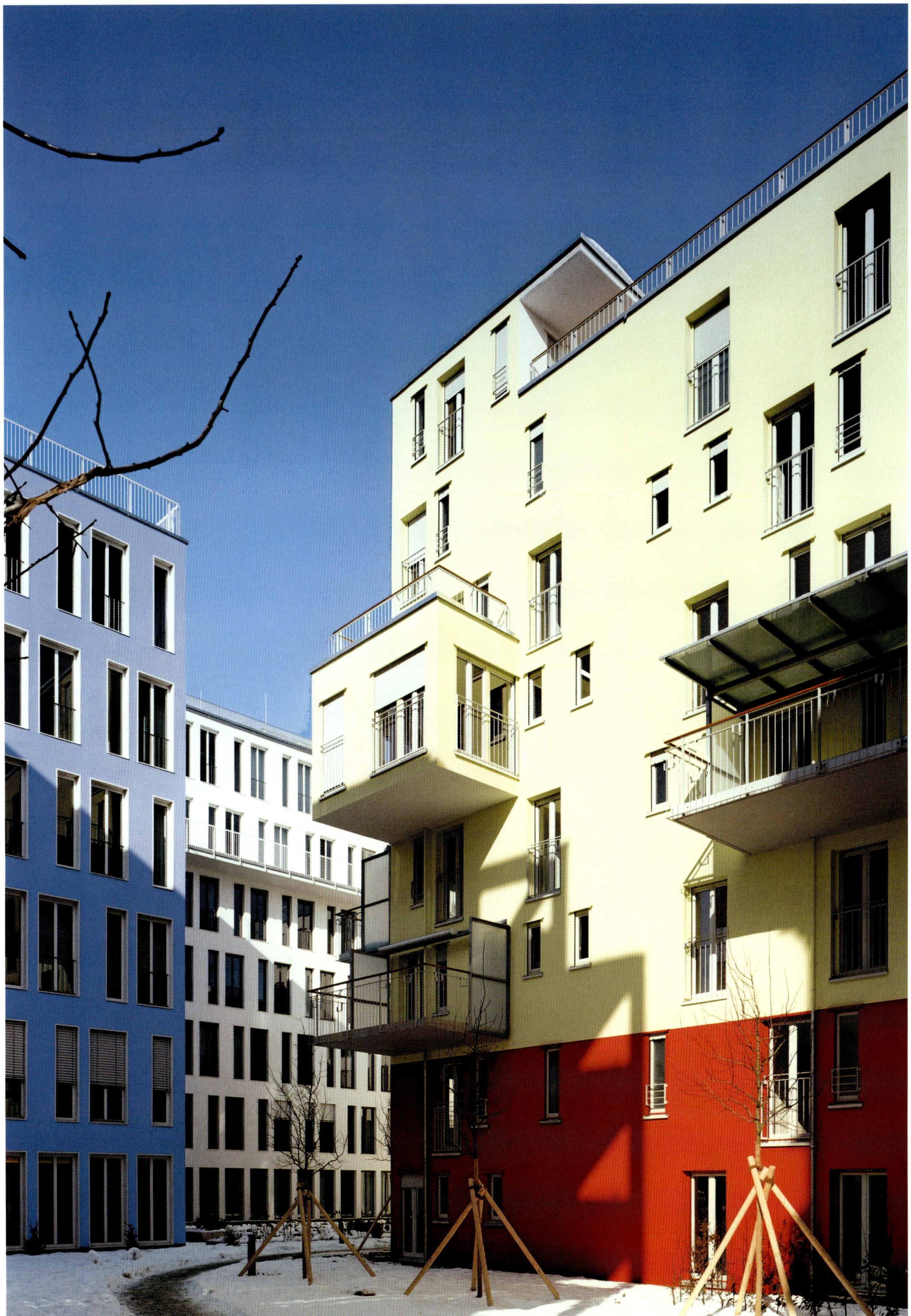

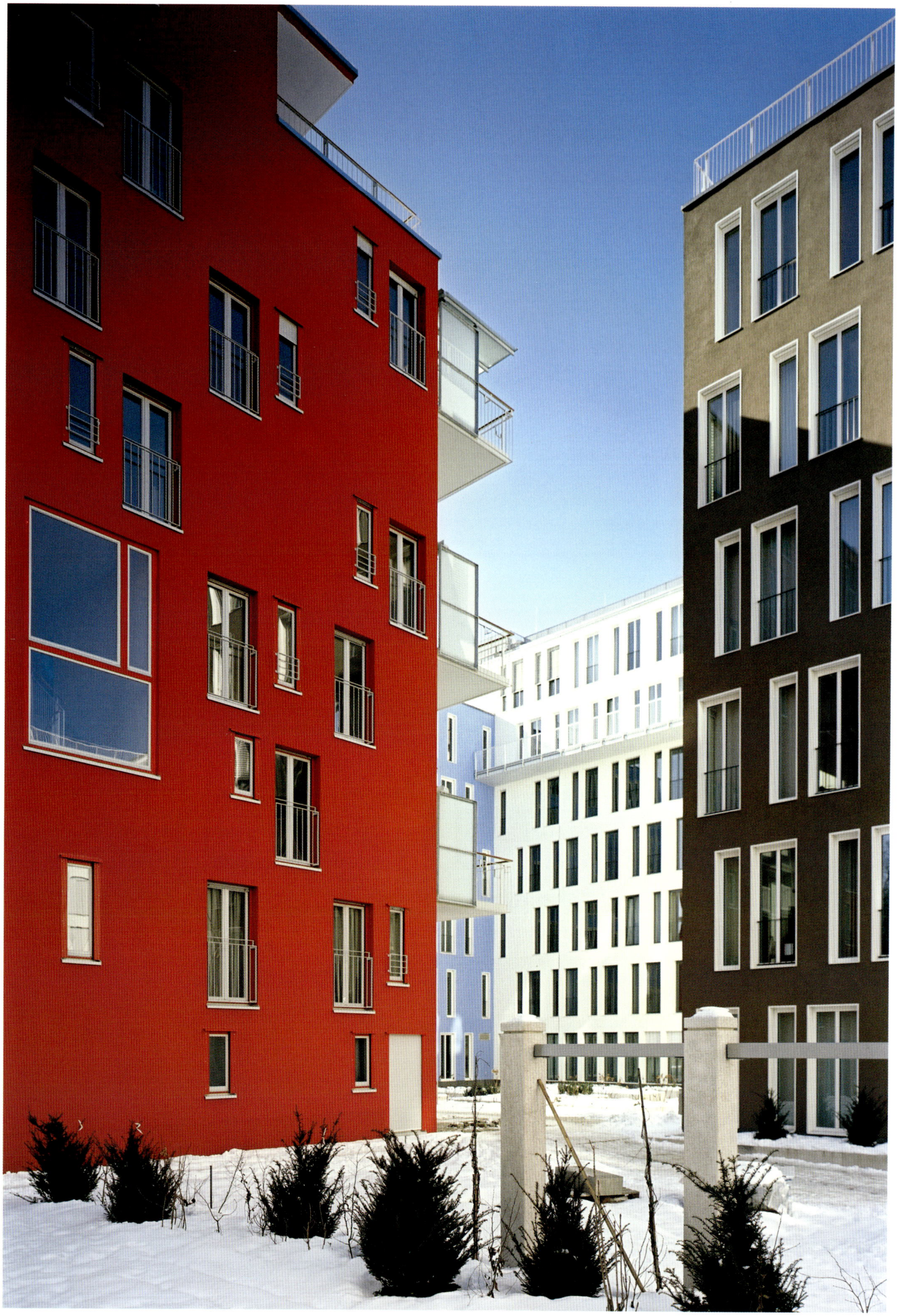

18. Blick von Nordosten. Von links nach rechts: Haus 6 (Steidle+Partner), Kontorhaus Süd.
19. Blick von Nordosten. Von links nach rechts: Haus 7 (Ortner & Ortner, Kontorhaus Süd, Haus 6 (Steidle+Partner).

18. View from northeast. From left to right: house 6 (Steidle+Partner), south office building.
19. View from northeast. From left to right: house 7 (Ortner & Ortner), south office building, house 6 (Steidle+Partner).

S. 46/47
20. Blick von Südosten. Von links nach rechts: Haus 4 (Hilmer & Sattler und Albrecht), Haus 3 (Hilmer & Sattler und Albrecht).

p. 46/47
20. View from the southeast. From left to right: house 4 (Hilmer & Sattler und Albrecht), house 3 (Hilmer & Sattler und Albrecht).

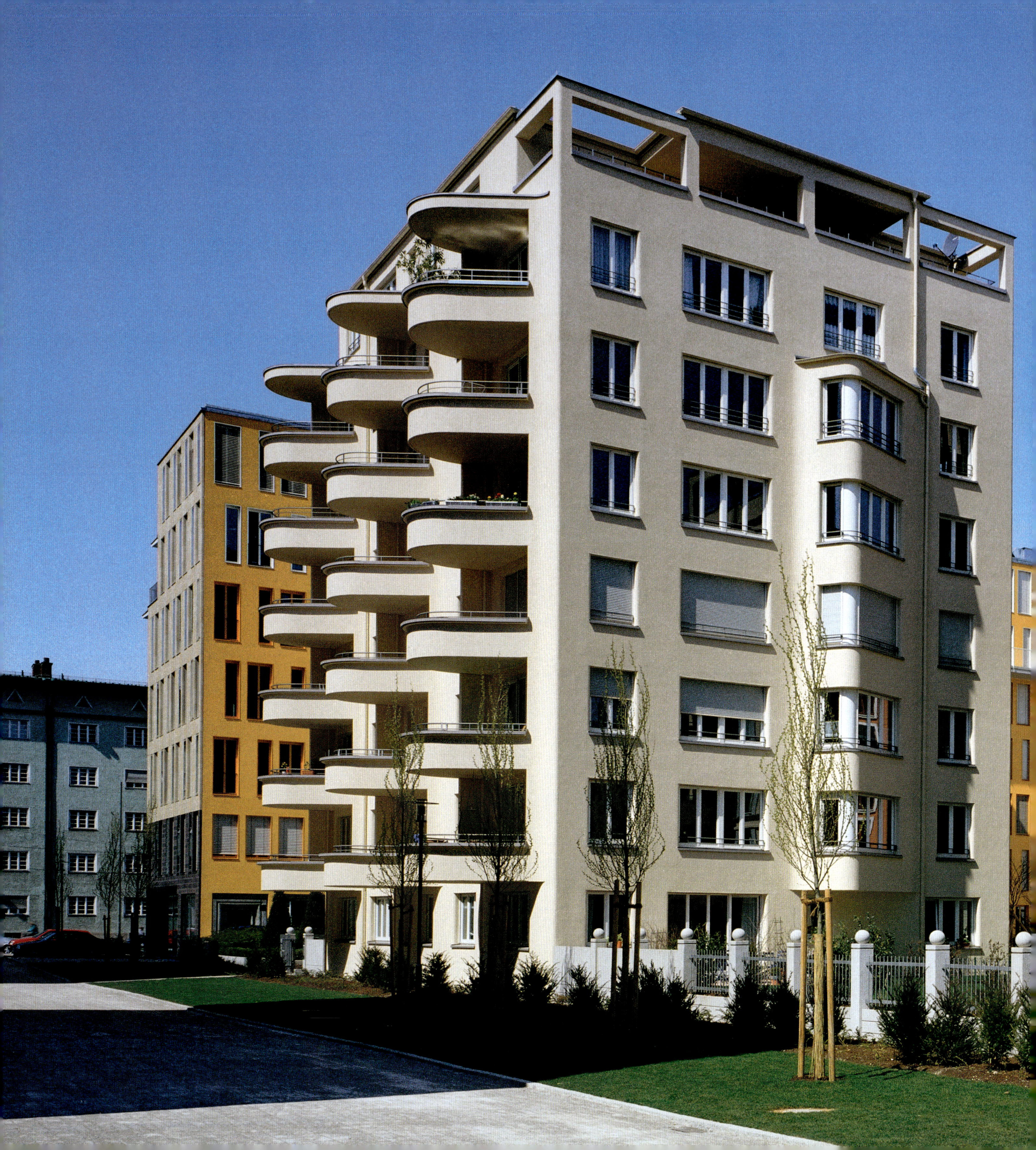

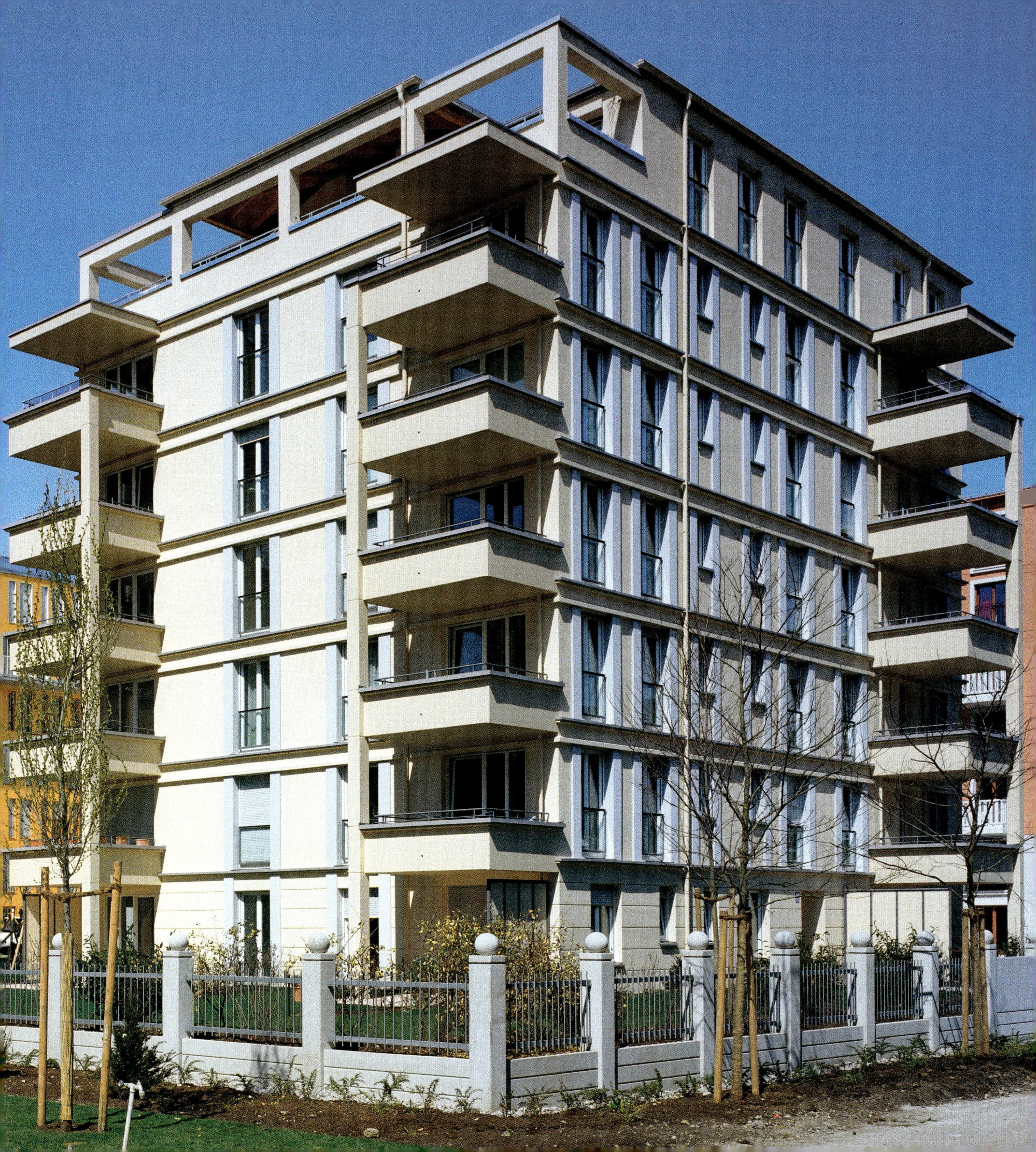

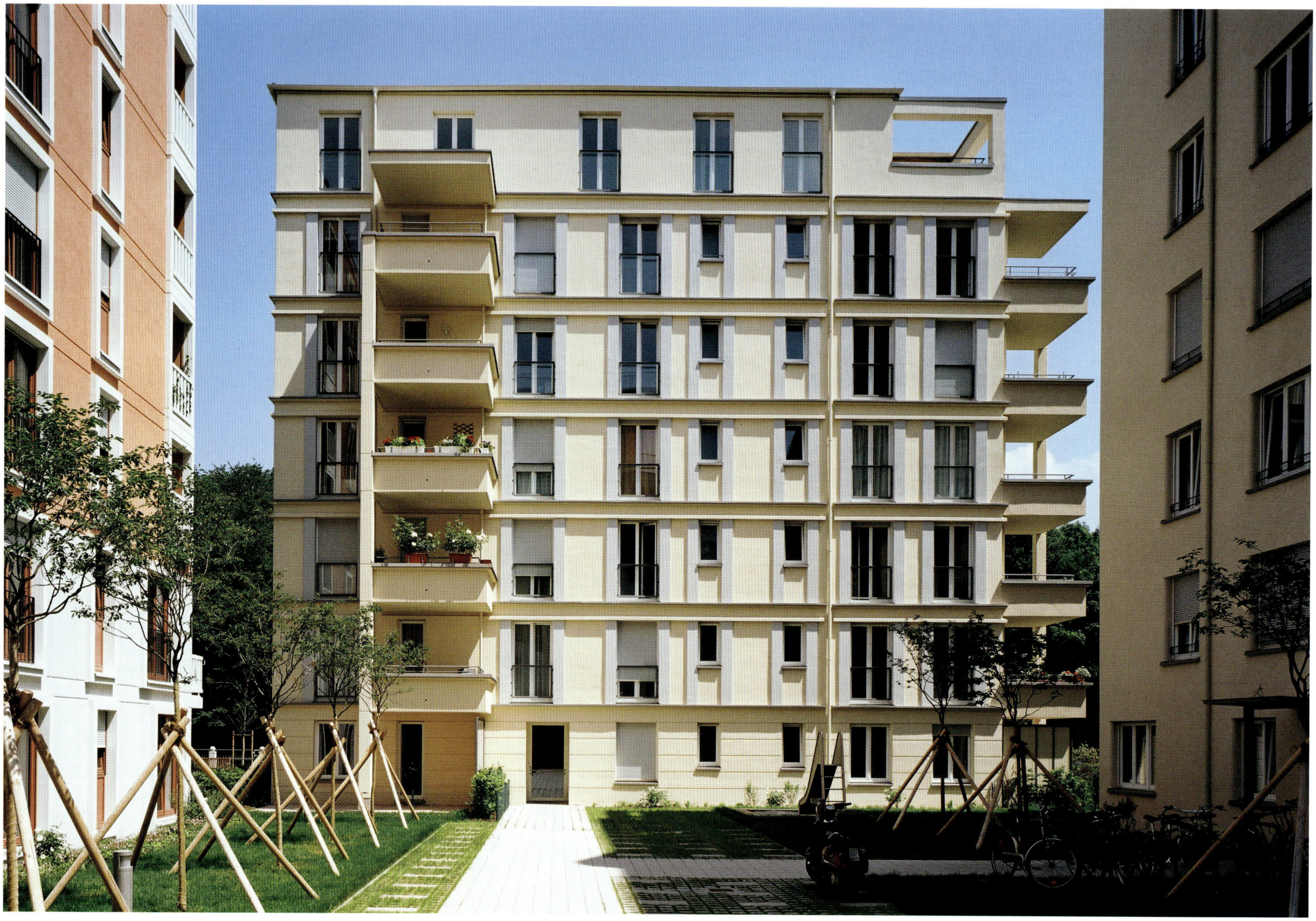

21. Blick von Westen. Von links nach rechts: Haus 2 (Ortner & Ortner), Haus 3 (Hilmer & Sattler und Albrecht), Haus 4 (Hilmer & Sattler und Albrecht).
22. Blick von Norden. Von links nach rechts: Haus 3 (Hilmer & Sattler und Albrecht), Haus 5 (Ortner & Ortner), Haus 4 (Hilmer & Sattler und Albrecht), Haus 2 (Ortner & Ortner).

21. View from the west. From left to right: house 2 (Ortner & Ortner), house 3 (Hilmer & Sattler und Albrecht), house 4 (Hilmer & Sattler und Albrecht).
22. View from the north. From left to right: house 3 (Hilmer & Sattler und Albrecht), house 5 (Ortner & Ortner), house 4 (Hilmer & Sattler und Albrecht), house 2 (Ortner & Ortner).

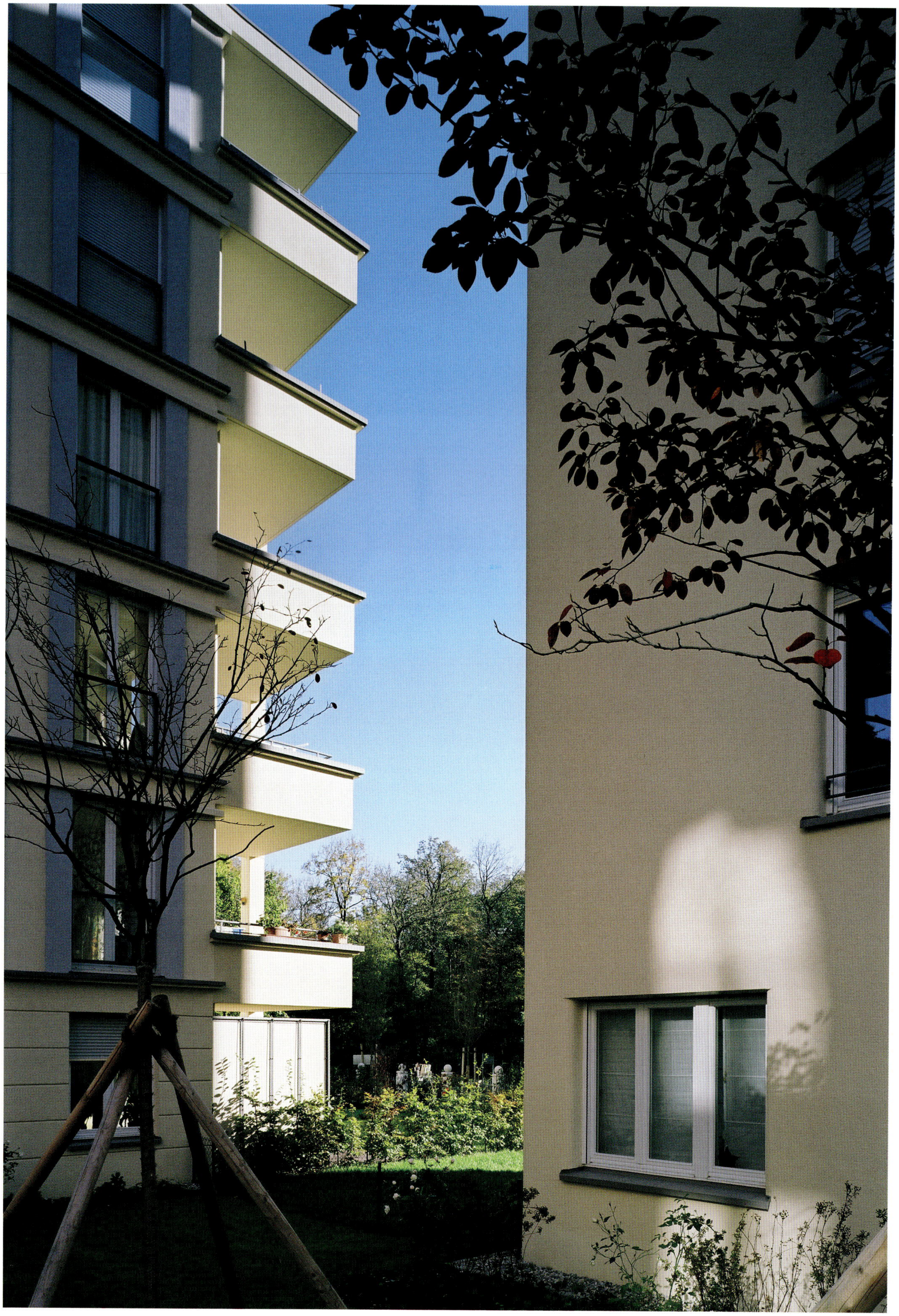

23. Blick von Nordwesten. Von links nach rechts: Haus 3 (Hilmer & Sattler und Albrecht), Haus 4 (Hilmer & Sattler und Albrecht).
24. Blick von Osten. Von links nach rechts: Kontorhaus Süd, Haus 4 (Hilmer & Sattler und Albrecht), Haus 3 (Hilmer & Sattler und Albrecht).

23. View from the northwest. From left to right: house 3 (Hilmer & Sattler und Albrecht), house 4 (Hilmer & Sattler und Albrecht).
24. View from the east. From left to right: south office building, house 4 (Hilmer & Sattler und Albrecht), house 3 (Hilmer & Sattler und Albrecht).

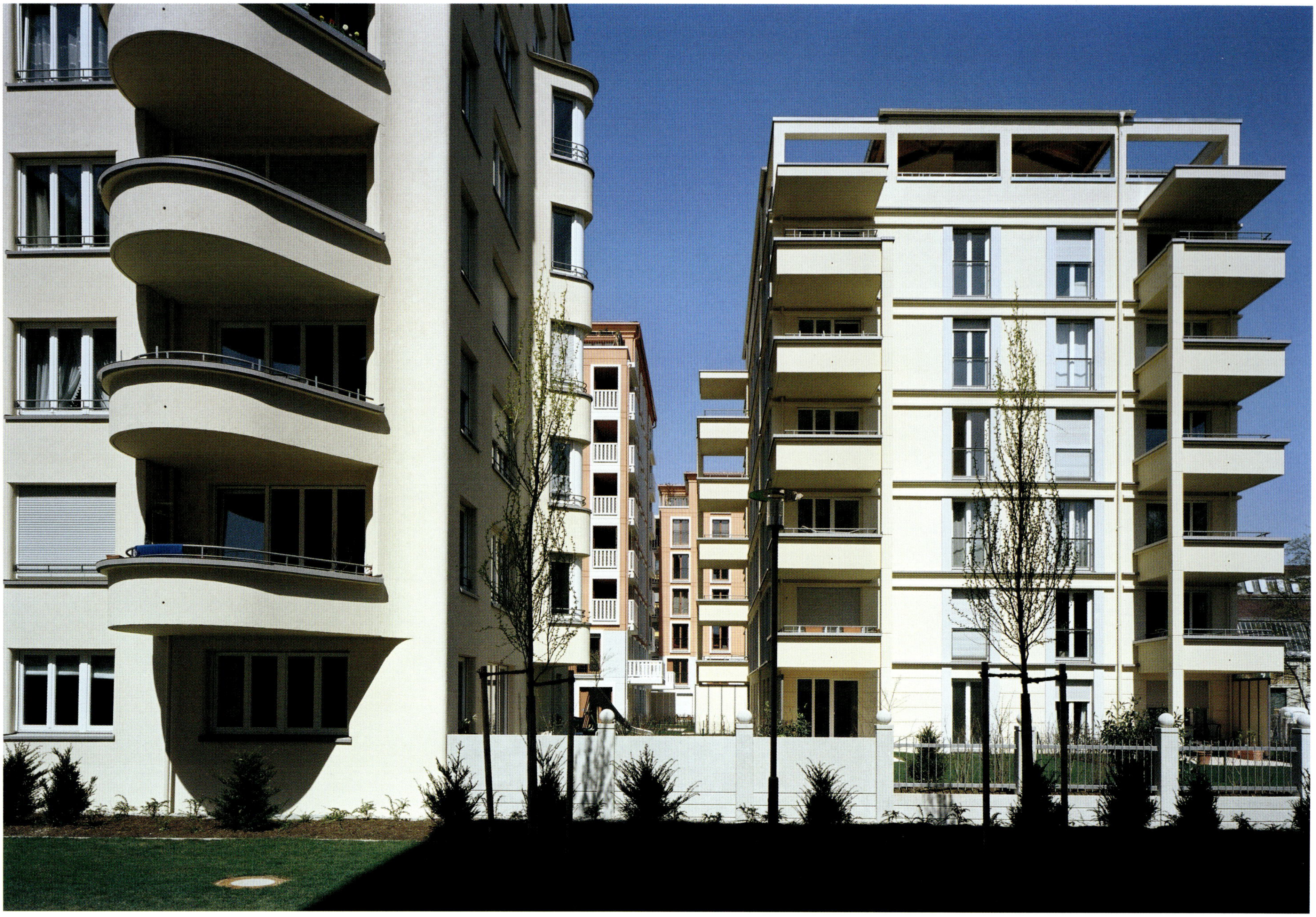

25. Blick von Süden. Von links nach rechts: Haus 4 (Hilmer & Sattler und Albrecht), Haus 2 (Ortner & Ortner), Haus 1 (Ortner & Ortner), Haus 3 (Hilmer & Sattler und Albrecht).
26. Blick von Südosten. Von links nach rechts: Kontorhaus Nord, Haus 4 (Hilmer & Sattler und Albrecht).
27. Blick von Südosten. Von links nach rechts: Haus 4 (Hilmer & Sattler und Albrecht), Kontorhaus Nord, Haus 3 (Hilmer & Sattler und Albrecht).

25. View from the south. From left to right: house 4 (Hilmer & Sattler und Albrecht), house 2 (Ortner & Ortner), house 1 (Ortner & Ortner), house 3 (Hilmer & Sattler und Albrecht).
26. View from the southeast. From left to right: north office building, house 4 (Hilmer & Sattler und Albrecht).
27. View from the southeast. From left to right: house 4 (Hilmer & Sattler und Albrecht), north office building, house 3 (Hilmer & Sattler und Albrecht).

28. Blick von Süden. Von links nach rechts: Haus 8 (Hilmer & Sattler und Albrecht), Haus 6 (Steidle+Partner), Haus 7 (Ortner & Ortner).
29. Blick von Westen. Von links nach rechts: Haus 6 (Steidle+Partner), Haus 7 (Ortner & Ortner), Haus 8 (Hilmer & Sattler und Albrecht).
30. Blick von Nordwesten. Von links nach rechts: Haus 5 (Ortner & Ortner), Haus 7 (Ortner & Ortner), Haus 6 (Steidle+Partner), Kontorhaus Süd.

28. View from the south. From left to right: house 8 (Hilmer & Sattler und Albrecht), house 6 (Steidle+Partner), house 7 (Ortner & Ortner).
29. View from the west. From left to right: house 6 (Steidle+Partner), house 7 (Ortner & Ortner), house 8 (Hilmer & Sattler und Albrecht).
30. View from the northwest. From left to right: house 5 (Ortner & Ortner), house 7 (Ortner & Ortner), house 6 (Steidle+Partner), south office building.

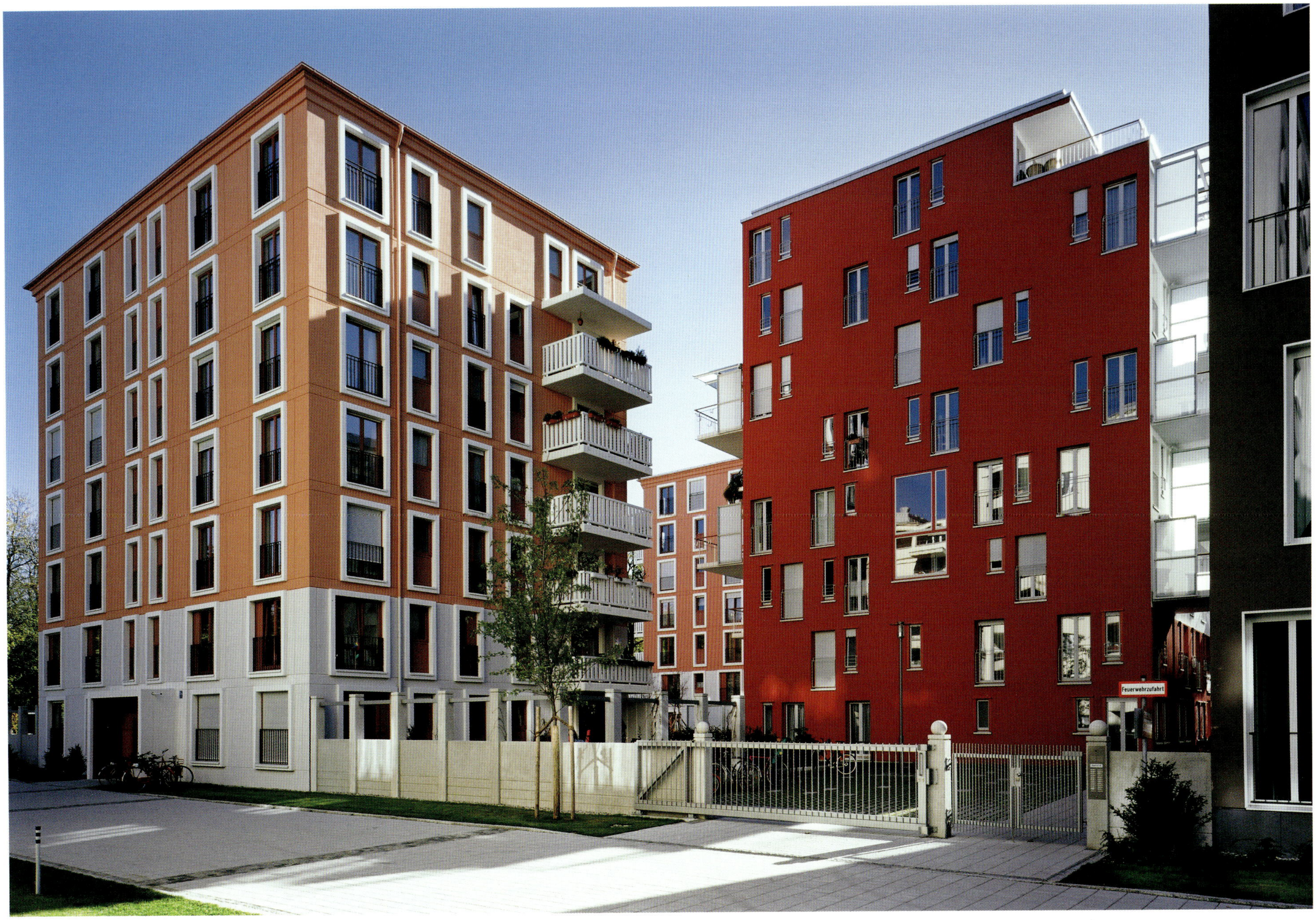
Feuerwehrzufahrt

31. Blick von Norden. Von links nach rechts: Haus 1 (Ortner & Ortner), Haus 2 (Ortner & Ortner), Kontorhaus Nord.
32. Blick von Westen. Von links nach rechts: Haus 1 (Ortner & Ortner), Haus 2 (Ortner & Ortner).

31. View from the north. From left to right: house 1 (Ortner & Ortner), house 2 (Ortner & Ortner), north office building
32. View from the west. From left to right: house 1 (Ortner & Ortner), house 2 (Ortner & Ortner).

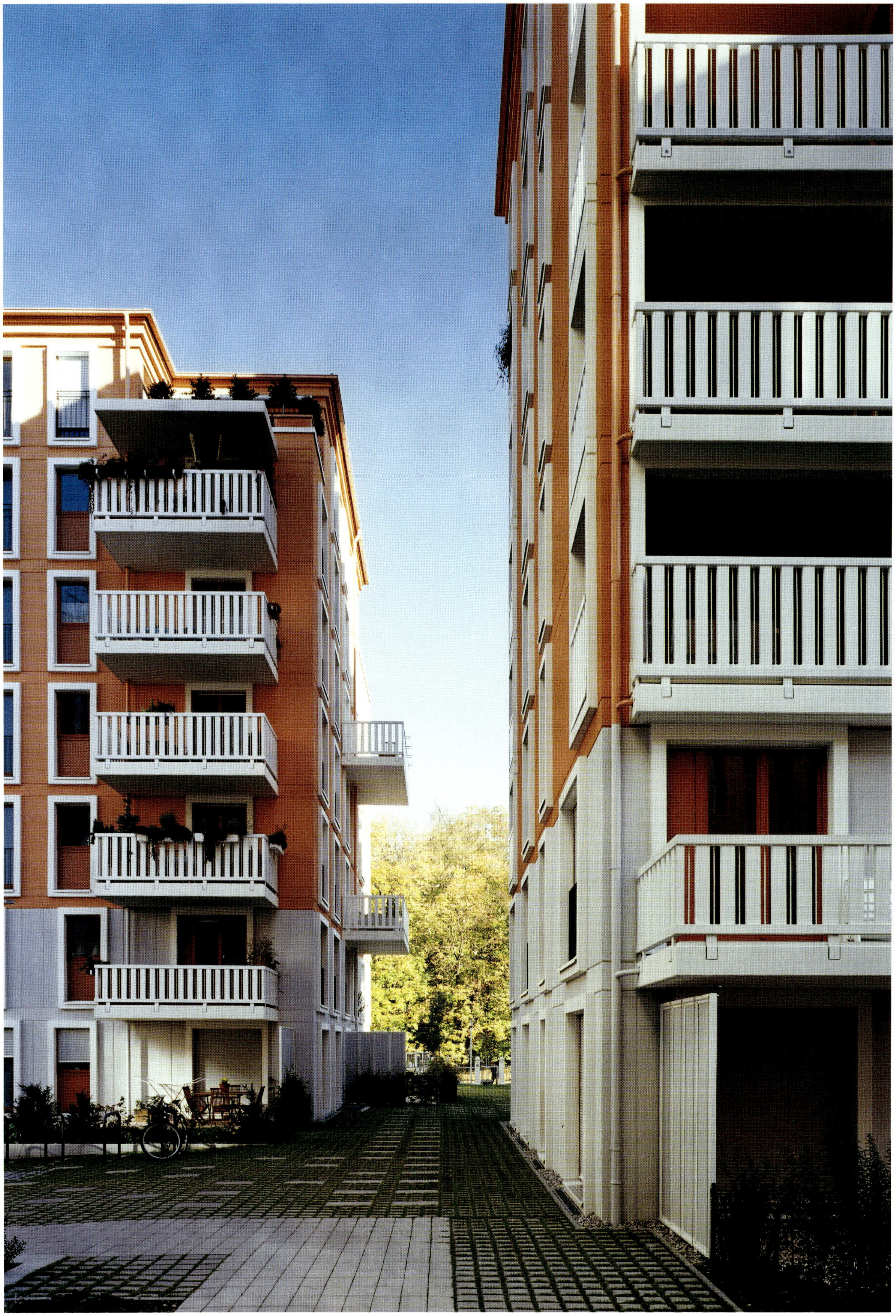

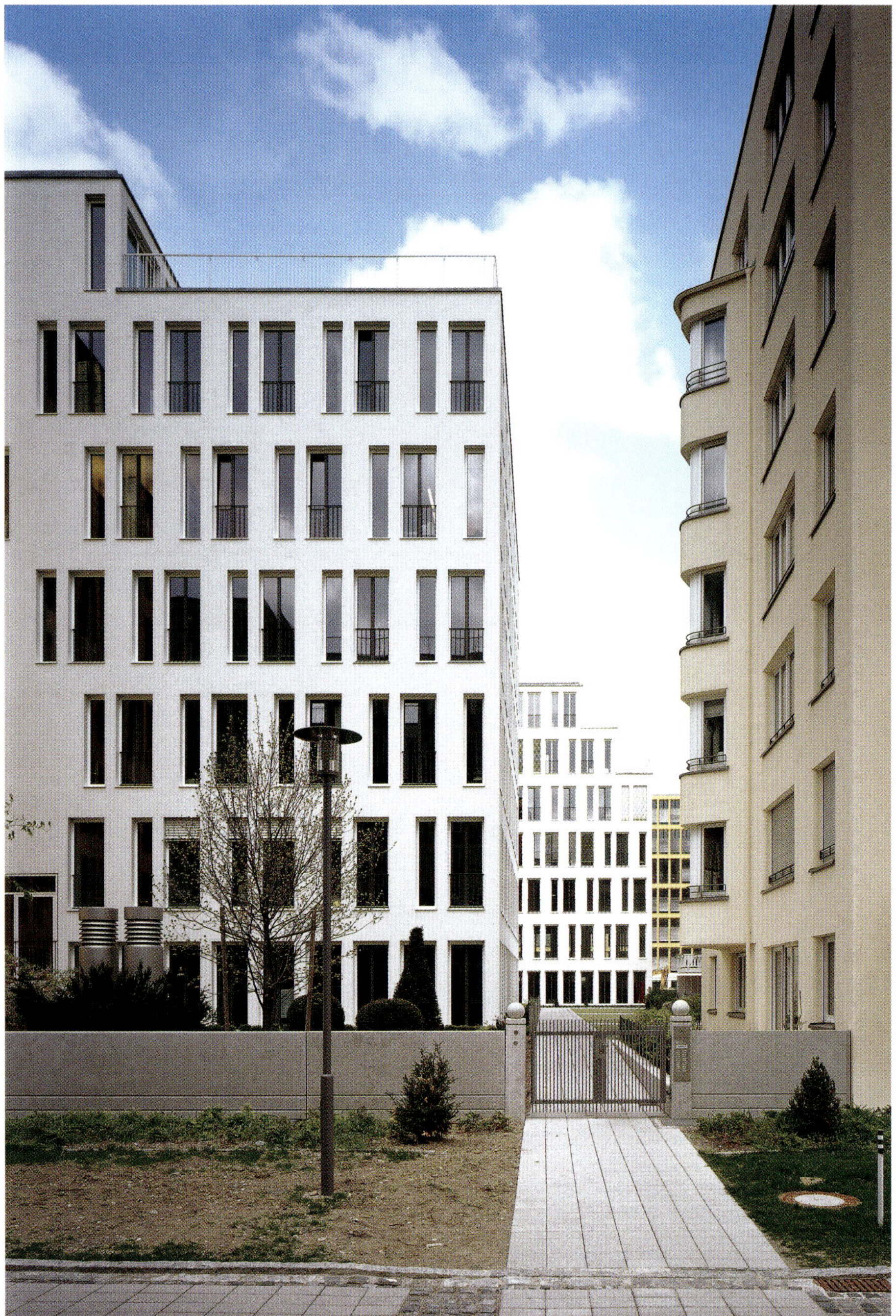

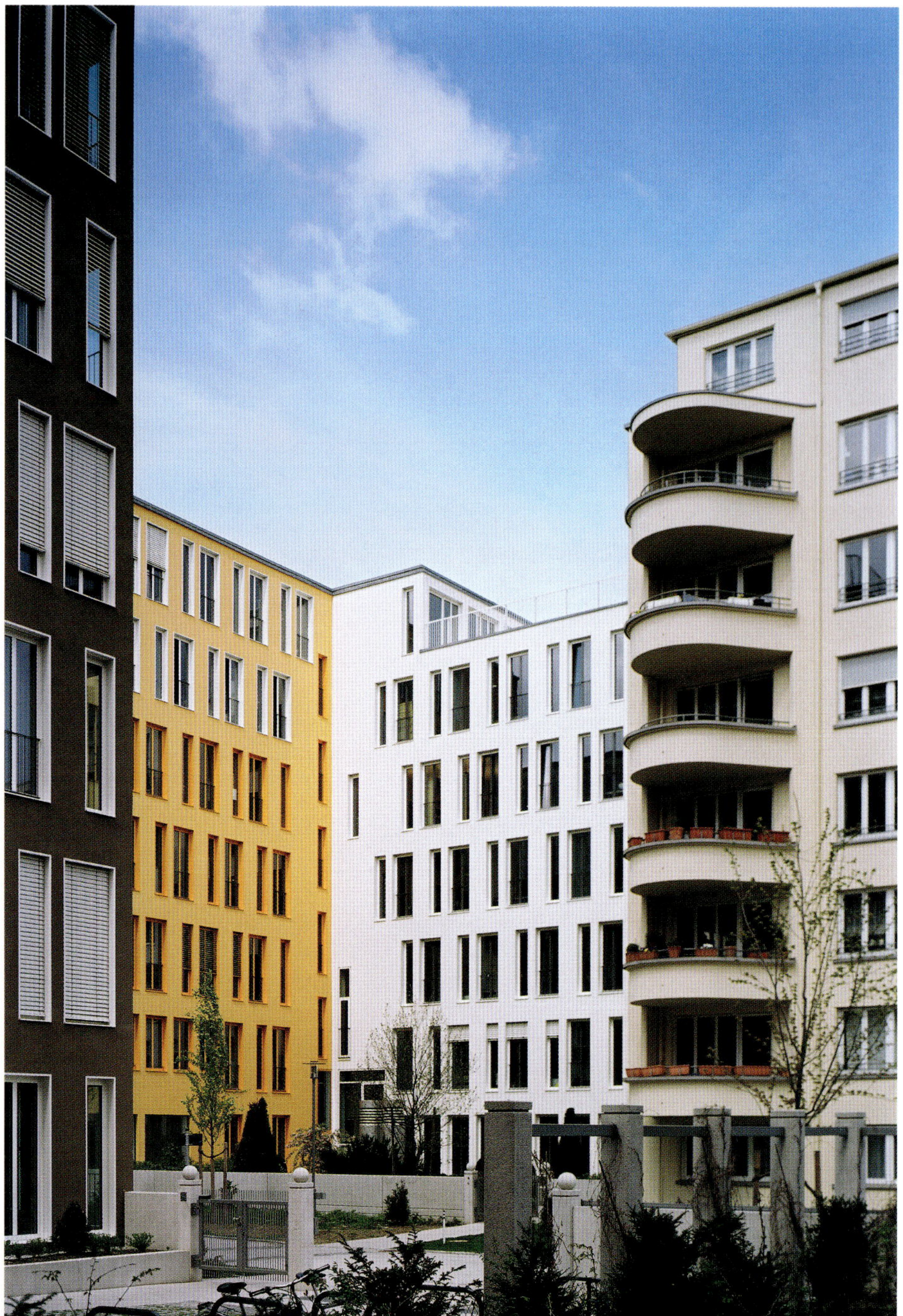

33. Blick von Osten. Von links nach rechts: Haus 6 (Steidle+Partner), Kontorhaus Süd.
34. Blick von Südosten. Von links nach rechts: Kontorhaus Nord, Haus 4 (Hilmer & Sattler und Albrecht).
35. Blick von Nordosten. Von links nach rechts: Kontorhaus Süd, Kontorhaus Nord.
36. Blick von Süden. Von links nach rechts: Kontorhaus Nord, Haus 4 (Hilmer & Sattler und Albrecht).

33. View from the east. From left to right: house 6 (Steidle+Partner), south office building.
34. View from the southeast. From left to right: north office building, house 4 (Hilmer & Sattler und Albrecht).
35. View from the northeast. From left to right: south office building, north office building.
36. View from the south. From left to right: north office building, house 4 (Hilmer & Sattler und Albrecht).

Am Bavariapark, München/Munich

Diese Publikation wurde von Otto Steidle angeregt und konzipiert. Während der Arbeit an dem Buch ist Otto Steidle unerwartet verstorben. Wir bedanken uns bei Ihm für die gemeinsame Zeit und für seine zahlreichen Anregungen.
This publication was initiated and prepared by Otto Steidle. While working on the book Otto Steidle unexpectedly passed away. We thank him for the time we could share with him and for his many suggestions.

Städtebaulicher Wettbewerb/Urban-design competition
1997

Masterplan
1997–2000

Entwurfs- und Bauzeit/Design and construction period
1999–2002

Projektentwicklung/Project development
Baywobau Bauträger AG, München/Munich; Weichinger Projektentwicklung GmbH GbR, München/Munich

Bauherren/Clients
Baywobau Bauträger AG, München/Munich; Weichinger Projektentwicklung GmbH GbR, München/Munich

Investoren/Investors
Kontorhaus Nord/North office building Ärzteversorgung Niedersachsen, Hannover/Hanover
Kontorhaus Süd/South office building Gerling Gesellschaft für Vermögensmanagement mbH, Köln/Cologne

Architekten/Architects
Städtebaulicher Wettbewerb und städtebauliche Planung/Urban-design competition and urban-design planning Steidle+Partner, München/Munich (Otto Steidle, Christian Kara, Nikolaus Hoffmann, Johann Spengler, Johannes Ernst)
Kontorhäuser/Office buildings Steidle+Partner, München/Munich (Otto Steidle, Johannes Ernst, Martin Klein, Alexandra Walz); CAD: vSTW Architekten, München/Munich
Wohngebäude 1, 2, 5, 7/Apartment buildings 1, 2, 5, 7 Ortner & Ortner Baukunst, Berlin (Projektleiter/Project manager: Thomas Emmrich; Mitarbeiter/Collaborators: Anne Niedeck, Stefan Bierik, Stefan Motz)
Wohngebäude 3, 4, 8/Apartment buildings 3, 4, 8 Hilmer & Sattler und Albrecht, München/Munich, Berlin (Projektleiter/Project manager: Daniel Türcke; Mitarbeiter/Collaborators: Daniel Kahala, Barbara Schindhelm); Werkpläne/Working drawings: Architekturbüro Bernd Obersteiner, München/Munich
Wohngebäude 6/Apartment building 6 Steidle+Partner, München/Munich (Otto Steidle, Astrid Dycka, Audrey Shimomura, Johannes Ernst)

Farbkonzepte und Glaskunst (Kontorhäuser und Wohngebäude 6)/Colour concepts and glass art (office buildings and apartment building 6)
Erich Wiesner, Berlin

Landschaftsplanung/Landscape planning
Gesamtentwurf Thomanek+Duquesnoy, Berlin (Projektarchitekten/Project architects: Claudia Liem, Ralph Meißner)
Werkpläne für den Bereich um die Wohnbauten/Working drawings for the area around the apartment buildings KLA Köster Landschaftsarchitektur, München/Munich

Tragwerksplanung/Structural engineering
Burggraf, Weichinger+Partner Ingenieurgesellschaft mbH, München/Munich (Projektleiter/Project manager: Werner Reiminger, Wolfram Summer)

Haustechnik (Kontorhäuser)/Mechanical engineering (office buildings)
Fischer & Fey Ingenieurgesellschaft mbH, München/Munich

Projektsteuerung/Project management
WPG Weichinger Projektentwicklung GmbH (Projektleiter/Project manager: Rolf Schroeder)

Bauleitung/Site management
BIP – Beratende Ingenieure für das Bauwesen VBI GmbH, München/Munich

Generalunternehmer/General contractor
WALTER BAU-AG vereinigt mit DYWIDAG, Niederlassung München/Munich branch (Projektleiter/Project manager: Matthias Häfner, Matthias Albert)

Die folgenden Firmen haben die Herausgabe dieses Buches finanziell unterstützt:
The following firms have given financial support to the publication of this book:

WPG Weichinger Projektentwicklung GmbH, München/Munich
Baywobau Bauträger AG, München/Munich
Gerling Gesellschaft für Vermögensmanagement mbH, Köln/Cologne
WALTER BAU-AG vereinigt mit DYWIDAG, Niederlassung München/Munich branch
GIMA Girnghuber GmbH & Co. KG, Marklkofen
Burggraf, Weichinger+Partner Ingenieurgesellschaft mbH, München/Munich